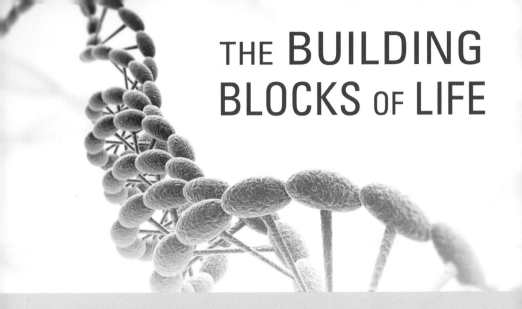

THE BUILDING
BLOCKS OF LIFE

EXAMINING
CELLS

Edited by **Louise Eaton** and **Kara Rogers**

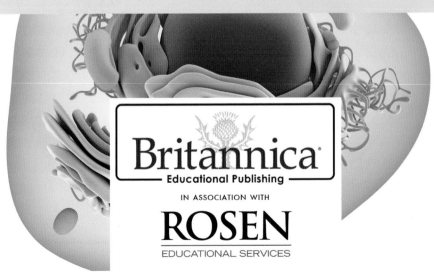

Britannica®
Educational Publishing

IN ASSOCIATION WITH

ROSEN
EDUCATIONAL SERVICES

Published in 2018 by Britannica Educational Publishing (a trademark of Encyclopædia Britannica, Inc.) in association with The Rosen Publishing Group, Inc.
29 East 21st Street, New York, NY 10010

Distributed exclusively by Rosen Publishing.
To see additional Britannica Educational Publishing titles, go to rosenpublishing.com.

Britannica Educational Publishing
J.E. Luebering: Executive Director, Core Editorial
Andrea R. Field: Managing Editor, Compton's by Britannica

Rosen Publishing
Meredith Day: Editor
Nelson Sá: Art Director
Brian Garvey: Series Designer
Ellina Litmanovich: Book Layout
Cindy Reiman: Photography Manager
Karen Huang: Photo Researcher

Library of Congress Cataloging-in-Publication Data

Names: Eaton, Louise, editor. | Rogers, Kara, editor.
Title: Examining cells / edited by Louise Eaton and Kara Rogers.
Description: New York : Britannica Educational Publishing in Association with Rosen Educational Services, 2018. | Series: The building blocks of life | Audience: Grades 9–12. | Includes bibliographical references and index.
Identifiers: LCCN 2017011649 | ISBN 9781538300077 (library bound : alk. paper)
Subjects: LCSH: Cells—Juvenile literature. | Cytology—Juvenile literature.
Classification: LCC QH582.5 .E93 2018 | DDC 571.6—dc23
LC record available at https://lccn.loc.gov/2017011649

Manufactured in Malaysia

Photo credits: Cover, p. 1 (DNA) Jezperklauzen/iStock/Thinkstock; cover. p. 1 (cell) Alfred Pasieka/Science Photo Library/Getty Images; p. 9 Andrew Brookes/Cultura/ Getty Images; p. 152 Ed Reschke/Photolibrary/Getty Images; p. 175 BONY/SIPA/ AP Images; p. 233 Science & Society Picture Library/Getty Images; p. 245 Georges Gobet/AFP/Getty Images; p. 253 Science Source. All other illustrations and diagrams Encyclopædia Britannica, Inc.

CONTENTS

CHAPTER 3

CHAPTER 4

CHAPTER 5

CHAPTER 6

INTRODUCTION

The smallest unit of living matter that can exist by itself is the cell. Some organisms, such as bacteria, consist of only a single cell. Others, such as humans and oak trees, are composed of many billions of cells. Cells exist in a variety of shapes and sizes. Red blood cells are disk-shaped, while some skin cells resemble cubes. A single cell could be as large as a tennis ball or so small that thousands would fit on the period at the end of this sentence. Regardless of size, however, every cell contains the components needed to maintain life. Cells normally function with great efficiency, though they are vulnerable to disease.

Cell size is usually measured in micrometers. A micrometer is equal to about one millionth of a meter, and about 25,000 micrometers equal 1 inch. The smallest bacteria are about 0.2 micrometer in diameter. The diameter of the average human cell is roughly 10 micrometer, making it barely visible without a microscope.

Based on fundamental differences in their cell structure, living organisms can be divided into two

This researcher is examining stem cells through an inverted microscope. Stem-cell research, though controversial, has the potential to transform cell biology and medicine.

major groups—prokaryotes and eukaryotes. Bacteria and archaea are prokaryotes. Animals, plants, fungi, and protists are eukaryotes.

Prokaryotic and eukaryotic cells are distinguished by several key characteristics. Both cell types contain DNA as their genetic material. However, prokaryotic DNA is single-stranded and circular and floats freely inside the cell; eukaryotic DNA is double-stranded and linear and is enclosed in a membrane-bound structure called the nucleus. Eukaryotes also have other specialized membrane-bound structures called organelles that do much of the cell's work.

Prokaryotes lack organelles, though they must accomplish many similar vital tasks. This inability to "delegate" tasks makes prokaryotes less metabolically efficient than eukaryotes.

All cells contain cytoplasm, a substance made up of water, proteins, and other molecules surrounded by a membrane. The cytoplasm of eukaryotic cells also contains numerous organelles. Much of the cell's work takes place in the cytoplasm. Water is the largest component of cytoplasm. Depending on the cell and its needs and conditions, water concentration varies from about 65 percent to roughly 95 percent. Suspended in the water are various solids such as proteins, carbohydrates, fat droplets, and pigments. As such, cytoplasm is a colloid rather than simply a solid or a liquid.

Cells can survive only in a liquid medium that brings in food and carries away waste. For unicellular (single-celled) organisms, such as bacteria, algae, and protozoa, this fluid can be an external body of water, such as a lake or stream. For multicellular (many-celled) organisms, however, the liquid medium is contained within the organism. In plants, for example, it is the sap; in animals, the blood and lymph.

The cell membrane is composed of two thin layers of phospholipid molecules studded with large proteins. Phospholipids are chemically related to fats and oils. Some of the membrane proteins are structural; others form pores that function as gateways to allow or prevent the transport of substances across the membrane.

Substances pass through the cell membrane in several ways. Small uncharged molecules, such as water, pass freely down their concentration gradient (from the side of the membrane where they are in higher concentration to the side of lower concentration). This movement is called diffusion. Other materials, such as ions (charged molecules) and certain other substances, must be transported across the membrane through channels—proteins embedded in the membrane, forming pores that are regulated by chemical signals from the cell. This process is called facilitated transport.

Endocytosis is another process used by cells to take in certain materials. The cell membrane forms a pocket around a substance in its environment. Inside the cell, the filled pocket breaks loose from the membrane, forming a bubblelike vacuole that drifts into the cytoplasm, where its contents are "digested": the vacuole wall is broken down and the contents are released into the cytoplasm. The reverse process, exocytosis, is used to remove material from the cell.

Virtually all prokaryotes, as well as the cells of plants, fungi, and some algae, have a cell wall—a rigid structure that surrounds the cell membrane. Most cell walls are composed of polysaccharides— long chains of sugar molecules linked by strong bonds. The cell wall helps maintain the cell's shape and enables larger organisms such as plants to grow upright. The cell wall also protects the cell against bursting under certain osmotic conditions.

Cells are constantly working to stay alive. Food molecules are changed into material needed for energy, and substances needed for growth and repair are synthesized, or manufactured. In eukaryotic cells most of these tasks take place inside membrane-bound bodies of the cytoplasm called organelles. According to the theory of endosymbiosis, certain organelles—in particular plastids (such as chloroplasts) and mitochondria—originated as small independent prokaryotic cells that invaded or were engulfed by primitive eukaryotic cells and formed an interdependent relationship with them.

The endoplasmic reticulum (ER), a network of membranous tubes and sacs, twists through the cytoplasm from the cell membrane to the membrane surrounding the nucleus. Located along portions of the endoplasmic reticulum are ribosomes, tiny bodies made of ribonucleic acid (RNA) that play a vital role in the manufacture of proteins. Ribosomes are also found scattered throughout the cytoplasm; distinct sets of ribosomes are found in plastids and mitochondria.

The Golgi complex, or Golgi apparatus, is a membranous structure composed of stacks of thin sacs. Newly made proteins and lipids move from the

ER to the Golgi complex. The materials are transported inside vesicles formed from the ER membrane. At the Golgi complex, the vesicles fuse with the Golgi membrane and the contents move inside the Golgi's lumen, or center, where they are further modified and subsequently stored. When the cell signals that certain proteins are needed, the latter are "packaged" by the Golgi for export—part of the Golgi membrane forms a vesicle that then buds off, or breaks away, from the larger apparatus. The vesicle may migrate to the cell membrane and export its contents via exocytosis or it may travel to an intracellular location if its contents are needed by the cell itself. Lipids are processed by the same methods.

Vacuoles are storage organelles that usually carry food molecules or wastes in solution. Lysosomes and peroxisomes are similar in appearance to vacuoles. Lysosomes are filled with enzymes that help the cell to digest large molecules, as well as old cell parts and foreign particles, such as bacteria. Peroxisomes contain enzymes that destroy toxic materials such as peroxide, which forms as an end product of some normal cellular activities. Lysosomes are produced in the Golgi complex; peroxisomes are self-replicating.

The centrosome is a spherical structure located near the nucleus of eukaryote cells. During the early phases of cell division, or mitosis, the centrosome replicates, resulting in two identical centrosomes that travel to opposite ends of the cell. In animal, fungal, and algal cells, the centrosomes contain a pair of structures called centrioles that produce microtubules. These tubules form a spindle that extends across the cell and helps the cell's chromosomes separate during cell division. Plant cells lack centrioles, but they do have centrosomes, which produce spindle fibers during cell division.

The cytoskeleton helps the cell maintain its shape, aids in cellular movement, and helps with internal movement. Found only in eukaryotic cells, the cytoskeleton is a network of protein filaments and tubules that extends throughout the cytoplasm. Microtubules help form structures such as cilia and flagella, which help single-celled organisms move, and the spindle fibers that move chromosomes during cell division. Microfilaments in the cytoskeleton give the cell its shape and help it contract; intermediate filaments give it strength.

Near the center of all eukaryotic cells is the nucleus. The nucleus is the control center of the cell and contains the chromosomes, which transmit hereditary traits. The nucleus usually has at least one nucleolus, a structure that is the site of RNA synthesis and storage. The nucleus is enclosed by a two-layered membrane and contains a syrupy nucleoplasm and strands of DNA wrapped around proteins in a manner that resembles a string of beads. Each strand contains a long series of genes—segments of DNA inherited from the previous generation. Genes determine the heritable characteristics of the organism. Genes also regulate cellular activities, including production of RNA, which in turn controls the manufacture of specific proteins. The DNA strands, which are called chromatin because they readily stain with dyes, are usually too thin to be seen with an optical microscope. When a cell is ready to divide, the chromatin–protein strands coil repeatedly around themselves, condensing into chromosomes.

Like all living things, cells have a life cycle—they begin, grow, maintain themselves, and reproduce. The cell cycle consists of two stages—one stage in which the cell grows and performs various life functions, and the other stage in which the cell divides, or reproduces itself.

While all cells divide, the process and purpose differs in unicellular and multicellular organisms. In unicellular organisms, cell division is one means of reproduction—prokaryotes and protists can produce new cells by undergoing simple fission, in which the cell divides after replicating its DNA. In multicellular organisms, cell division is more complex. For somatic cells (any cell type except germ cells), it is a means of growth and repair. Germ cells (those that give rise to sperm, eggs, and pollen) undergo a special type of cell division called meiosis as part of reproduction.

Some cells in multicellular organisms are modified to carry out a particular function, such as transporting a certain substance or executing a specific task. These cells are called specialized cells. While they have most of the same features as other cells, specialized cells have special structural adaptations that help them do their respective jobs. Root hair cells, palisade cells, and guard cells are examples of specialized plant cells.

Animals have many kinds of specialized cells. Red blood cells, which transport oxygen from the lungs to all of the body's tissues, contain hemoglobin, an iron-rich protein that binds oxygen. The cells are small and highly flexible, which helps them squeeze through even the smallest blood vessels, and their biconcave shape allows for oxygen exchange at a constant rate.

The male's sperm and the female's ova (eggs) are also specialized cells. Sperm cells have a tail, or flagellum, that helps propel them up the female reproductive tract to find an egg to fertilize. The sperm's head contains special enzymes that help it penetrate the egg cell at fertilization. Egg cells are large and contain abundant nutrient-rich cytoplasm that will help nourish the developing zygote after fertilization.

Cells were first described by the English scientist Robert Hooke, who in 1665 published a book about his findings. Hooke had sliced thin sections of cork to view under a microscope of his own design. He was able to see the minute, boxlike units of which the cork was made up. Hooke called these structures cells because he thought the boxes looked like monastery cells. The first description of living cells was provided in 1674 by Dutch scientist Antonie van Leeuwenhoek, who observed bacteria and protozoa under his microscope. Ten years later Leeuwenhoek gave the first accurate description of red blood cells.

Improvements in microscopes by the 19th century allowed more detailed investigations. In the 1830s Scottish botanist Robert Brown discovered the cell nucleus, and two German scientists, Matthias J. Schleiden and Theodor Schwann, concluded independently that cells were the basis of all life, a view called the cell theory. Rudolf Virchow, another German scientist, stated in 1858 that all cells develop from previously existing cells. During the late 19th century, techniques of fixing and staining tissues to preserve cells opened the way for intensive research.

Scientists use a variety of microscopes to study cells. An optical, or light, microscope uses a beam of light and optical lenses for viewing a specimen. A bright-field optical microscope, in which the background is brightly lit, can achieve a power of magnification of about 1,000. Electron microscopes, which were first developed in the early 20th century, use magnetic fields to control a beam of electrons (negatively charged particles) to get an image. Electron microscopes can produce an image with a power of magnification of up to one million, allowing biologists to examine the structure and contents of cells at an extremely fine scale.

Stem cells, which have the ability to reproduce and form specialized cells of various tissues and organs, potentially could be used to treat a variety of physical disorders and injuries, such as Alzheimer disease, Parkinson disease, heart disease, diabetes, and damage to the spinal cord. Researchers also use stem cells in experiments to study diseases, genes, and cell functioning and to test possible new medicines. There are two major types of stem cells: embryonic stem cells and adult stem cells. Until recently it was thought that embryonic stem cells could be obtained only from human embryos, which stirred much debate. In the first decade of the 21st century, researchers found a way to create these cell lines from adult cells, such as cells of the skin. Research into the behavior and function of different types of cells can provide great insight into biology, chemistry, and medicine.

CELL ORGANIZATION AND EVOLUTION

C ells are basic membrane-bound units that contain the fundamental molecules of life. All living things are composed of cells. A single cell is often a complete organism in itself, such as a bacterium or yeast. Other cells acquire specialized functions as they mature. These cells cooperate with other specialized cells and become the building blocks of large multicellular organisms—such as animals, including humans.

A cell functions both as an individual unit and as a contributing part of a larger organism. As an individual unit, the cell is capable of metabolizing its own nutrients, synthesizing many types of molecules, providing its own energy, and replicating itself to produce succeeding generations. It can be viewed as an enclosed vessel, within which innumerable chemical reactions take place simultaneously. These reactions are under precise control so that

Some typical cells

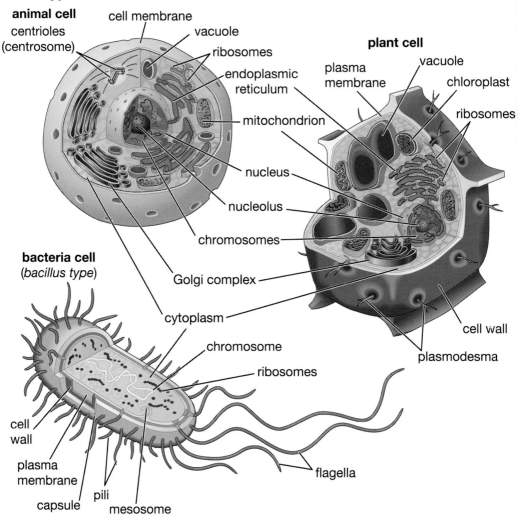

animal cell
centrioles (centrosome)
cell membrane
vacuole
ribosomes
endoplasmic reticulum
mitochondrion
nucleus
nucleolus
chromosomes
Golgi complex
cytoplasm

plant cell
plasma membrane
vacuole
chloroplast
ribosomes
cell wall
plasmodesma

bacteria cell
(*bacillus type*)
chromosome
ribosomes
cell wall
plasma membrane
capsule
pili
mesosome
flagella

© 2012 Encyclopædia Britannica, Inc.

Animal cells and plant cells contain membrane-bound organelles, including a distinct nucleus. In contrast, bacterial cells do not contain organelles.

they contribute to the life and procreation of the cell. In a multicellular organism, cells become specialized to perform different functions through the process of differentiation. To do this, each cell keeps in constant communication with its neighbours. As it receives nutrients from and expels wastes into its surroundings, it adheres to and cooperates with other cells. Cooperative assemblies of similar cells form tissues, and a cooperation between tissues in turn forms organs, which carry out the functions necessary to sustain the life of an organism.

EUKARYOTES VERSUS PROKARYOTES

Eukaryotes and prokaryotes are groups of organisms that are distinguished by fundamental differences in their cell plans. A eukaryote is any cell or organism that possesses a clearly defined nucleus. The eukaryotic cell has a nuclear membrane that surrounds the nucleus, in which the well-defined chromosomes (bodies containing the hereditary material) are located. Eukaryotic cells also contain organelles, including mitochondria (cellular energy exchangers), a Golgi apparatus (secretory device), an endoplasmic reticulum (a canal-like system of membranes within the cell), and lysosomes (digestive apparatus within many cell types).

A prokaryote is any organism that lacks a distinct nucleus and other organelles because of the absence

Animal cell

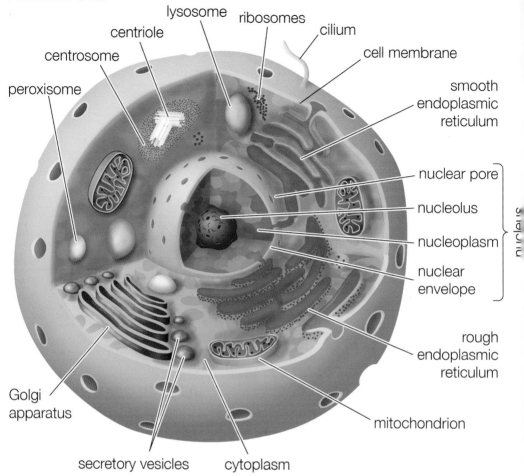

lysosome ribosomes
centriole cilium
centrosome cell membrane
peroxisome smooth endoplasmic reticulum
nuclear pore
nucleolus
nucleoplasm
nuclear envelope
rough endoplasmic reticulum
Golgi apparatus
mitochondrion
secretory vesicles cytoplasm

nucleus

Cutaway drawing of a eukaryotic cell, indicating various organelles and parts of the nucleus

of internal membranes. Bacteria are among the best-known prokaryotic organisms. The lack of internal membranes in prokaryotes distinguishes them from eukaryotes. The prokaryotic cell membrane is made up of phospholipids and constitutes the cell's primary osmotic barrier. The cytoplasm contains ribosomes, which carry out protein synthesis, and a double-stranded deoxyribonucleic acid (DNA) chromosome, which is usually circular. Many prokaryotes also contain additional circular DNA molecules called plasmids, with additional dispensable cell functions, such as encoding proteins to inactivate antibiotics. Some prokaryotes have flagella. Prokaryotic flagella are distinct in design and movement from the flagella found on some eukaryotes.

NATURE AND FUNCTION OF CELLS

A cell is enclosed by a plasma membrane, which forms a selective barrier that allows nutrients to enter and waste products to leave. The genetic material of cells contains the information necessary for cell growth and reproduction. Each eukaryotic cell contains only one nucleus, whereas other types of organelles are present in multiple copies in the cellular contents, or cytoplasm. These other organelles perform specific functions. For example, mitochondria are responsible for the energy transactions necessary for cell survival, lysosomes digest unwanted materials within the cell, and the endoplasmic reticulum and the Golgi apparatus play important roles in the internal organization of the cell by synthesizing selected molecules and then processing, sorting, and directing them to their proper locations. In addition, plant cells contain chloroplasts, which are responsible for photosynthesis, whereby the energy of sunlight is used to convert molecules of carbon dioxide (CO_2) and water (H_2O) into carbohydrates.

Between all these organelles is the space in the cytoplasm called the cytosol. The cytosol contains an organized framework of fibrous molecules that constitute the cytoskeleton, which gives a cell its shape, enables organelles to move within the cell, and provides a mechanism by which the cell itself can move. The cytosol also contains more than 10,000 different kinds of molecules that are involved in cellular biosynthesis, the process of making large biological molecules from small ones. Although specialized organelles are a characteristic of cells of eukaryotes and are absent from prokaryotes, all cells share strong similarities in biochemical function.

Cells contain a special collection of molecules that are enclosed by a membrane. These molecules give cells the ability to grow and reproduce. The overall process of cellular reproduction occurs in two steps: cell growth and cell division. During cell growth, the cell ingests certain molecules from its surroundings by selectively carrying them through its cell membrane. Once inside the cell, these molecules are subjected to the action of highly specialized, large, elaborately folded molecules called enzymes.

Enzymes act as catalysts by binding to ingested molecules and regulating the rate at which they are

DISCOVERING CELLULAR STRUCTURES

Belgian-American cytologist Albert Claude (1898–1983) developed the principal methods of separating and analyzing components of the living cell. For this work, on which modern cell biology is partly based, Claude, his student George Palade, and Christian de Duve shared the Nobel Prize for Physiology or Medicine in 1974.

In attempting to isolate the Rous sarcoma virus from chicken tumours, Claude spun cell extracts containing the virus in centrifuges that concentrated heavier particles in the bottom of the test tube; lighter particles settled in layers above. For comparison, he began centrifuging normal cells. This centrifugal separation of the cell components made possible a biochemical analysis of them that confirmed that the separated particles consisted of distinct organelles. Such analysis enabled Claude to discover the endoplasmic reticulum (a membranous network within cells) and to clarify the function of the mitochondria as the centres of respiratory activity.

Claude turned in 1942 to the electron microscope—an instrument that had not been used in biological research—looking first at separated components, then at whole cells. His demonstration of the instrument's usefulness in this regard eventually helped scientists to correlate the biological activity of each cellular component with its structure and its place in the cell.

(Continued on the next page)

(Continued from the previous page)

Palade performed many studies on the internal organization of such cell structures as mitochondria, chloroplasts, the Golgi apparatus, and others. His most important discovery was that microsomes, bodies formerly thought to be fragments of mitochondria, are actually parts of the endoplasmic reticulum (internal cellular transport system) and have a high ribonucleic acid (RNA) content. They were subsequently named ribosomes.

De Duve discovered lysosomes (the digestive organelles of the cell) and peroxisomes (organelles that are the site of metabolic processes involving hydrogen peroxide). His discovery of lysosomes arose out of his research on the enzymes involved in the metabolism of carbohydrates by the liver. While using Claude's technique of separating the components of cells by spinning them in a centrifuge, he noticed that the cells' release of an enzyme called acid phosphatase increased in proportion to the amount of damage done to the cells during centrifugation. De Duve reasoned that the acid phosphatase was enclosed within the cell in some kind of membranous envelope that formed a self-contained organelle. He calculated the probable size of this organelle, christened it the lysosome, and later identified it in electron microscope pictures. De Duve's discovery of lysosomes answered the question of how the powerful enzymes used by cells to digest nutrients are kept separate from other cell components.

chemically altered. These chemical alterations make the molecules more useful to the cell. Unlike the ingested molecules, catalysts are not chemically altered themselves during the reaction, allowing one catalyst to regulate a specific chemical reaction in many molecules.

Cells are largely composed of compounds that contain carbon. The study of how carbon atoms interact with other atoms in molecular compounds forms the basis of the field of organic chemistry and plays a large role in understanding the basic functions of cells. Because carbon atoms can form stable bonds with four other atoms, they are uniquely suited for the construction of complex molecules. These complex molecules are typically made up of chains and rings that contain hydrogen, oxygen, and nitrogen atoms, as well as carbon atoms. These molecules may consist of anywhere from 10 to millions of atoms linked together in specific arrays.

Most, but not all, carbon-containing molecules in cells are built up from members of one of four different families of small organic molecules: sugars, amino acids, nucleotides, and fatty acids. Each of these families contains a group of molecules that resemble one another in both structure and function. In addition to other important functions, these molecules are used to build large macromolecules. For example, the sugars can be linked to form polysaccharides such as starch and glycogen, the amino

Approximate Chemical Composition of a Typical Mammalian Cell	
component	percentage of total cell weight
water	69.65
inorganic ions (sodium, potassium, magnesium, calcium, chloride, etc.)	1
miscellaneous small metabolites	3
proteins	18
RNA	1.1
DNA	0.25
phospholipids and other lipids	5
polysaccharides	2

acids can be linked to form proteins, the nucleotides can be linked to form the DNA and RNA (ribonucleic acid) of chromosomes, and the fatty acids can be linked to form the lipids of all cell membranes.

Most of the catalytic macromolecules in cells are enzymes, and most enzymes are proteins. Key to the catalytic property of an enzyme is its tendency to undergo a change in its shape when it binds to its substrate, thus bringing together reactive groups on substrate molecules. Some enzymes are macromolecules of RNA, called ribozymes. Ribozymes consist of linear chains of nucleotides that fold in specific ways to form unique surfaces, similar to the ways in which proteins fold. As with proteins, the specific sequence of nucleotide subunits in an RNA chain gives each macromolecule a unique character. RNA molecules are much less frequently used as catalysts in cells than are protein molecules, presumably because proteins, with the greater variety of amino acid side chains, are more diverse and capable of complex shape changes. However, RNA molecules are thought to have preceded protein molecules during evolution and to have catalyzed most of the chemical reactions required before cells could evolve.

COUPLED CHEMICAL REACTIONS

Cells must obey the laws of chemistry and thermodynamics. When two molecules react with each other inside a cell, their atoms are rearranged, forming different molecules as reaction products and releasing or consuming energy in the process. Overall, chemical reactions occur only in one direction. That is, the final reaction product molecules cannot spontaneously react, in a reversal of the original process, to reform the original molecules. This directionality of chemical reactions is explained by the fact that molecules only change from states of higher free energy to states of lower free energy. Free energy is the ability to perform work (in this case, the "work" is the rearrangement of atoms in the chemical reaction). When work is performed, some free energy is used and lost, with the result that the process ends at lower free energy. To use a familiar mechanical analogy, water at the top of a hill has the ability to perform the "work" of flowing downhill (i.e., it has high free energy), but, once it has flowed downhill, it cannot flow back up (i.e., it is in a state of low free energy). However, through another work process— that of a pump, for example—the water can be returned to the top of the hill, thereby recovering its ability to flow downhill. In thermodynamic terms, the free energy of the water has been increased by energy from an outside source (i.e., the pump). In the same way, the product molecules of a chemical reaction in a cell cannot reverse the reaction and return to their original state unless energy is supplied by coupling the process to another chemical reaction.

All catalysts, including enzymes, accelerate chemical reactions without affecting their direction. To return to the mechanical analogy, enzymes cannot make water flow uphill, although they can provide specific pathways for a downhill flow. Yet most of the chemical reactions that the cell needs to synthesize new molecules necessary for its growth require an uphill flow. In other words, the reactions require more energy than their starting molecules can provide.

Cells use a single strategy over and over again in order to get around the limitations of chemistry: they use the energy from an energy-releasing chemical reaction to drive an energy-absorbing reaction that would otherwise not occur. A useful mechanical analogy might be a mill wheel driven by the water in a stream. To flow downhill, the water is forced to flow past the blades of the wheel, causing the wheel to turn. In this way, part of the energy from the moving stream is harnessed to move a mill wheel, which may be linked to a winch. As the winch turns, it can be used to pull a heavy load uphill. Thus, the energy-absorbing (but useful) uphill movement of a load can be driven by coupling it directly to the energy-releasing flow of water.

In cells, enzymes play the role of mill wheels by coupling energy-releasing reactions with energy-absorbing reactions. In cells the most important energy-releasing reaction serving a role similar to that of the flowing stream is the hydrolysis of adenosine triphosphate (ATP). In turn, the production of ATP molecules in the cells is an energy-absorbing reaction that is driven by being coupled to the energy-releasing breakdown of sugar molecules. In retracing this chain of reactions, it is necessary first to understand the source of the sugar molecules.

PHOTOSYNTHESIS

Sugar molecules are produced by the process of photosynthesis in plants and certain bacteria. These organisms lie at the base of the food chain, in that animals and other nonphotosynthesizing organisms depend on them for a constant supply of life-supporting organic molecules. Humans, for example, obtain these molecules by eating plants or other organisms that have previously eaten food derived from photosynthesizing organisms.

Plants and photosynthetic bacteria are unique in their ability to convert the freely available electromagnetic energy in sunlight into chemical bond energy, the energy that holds atoms together in molecules and is transferred or released in chemical reactions. The process of photosynthesis can be summarized by the following equation:

$$\text{(solar) energy} + CO_2 + H_2O \rightarrow \text{sugar molecules} + O_2.$$

The energy-absorbing photosynthetic reaction is the reverse of the energy-releasing oxidative decomposition of sugar molecules. During photosynthesis, chlorophyll molecules absorb energy from sunlight and use it to fuel the production of simple sugars and other carbohydrates. The resulting abundance of sugar molecules and related biological products makes possible the existence of nonphotosynthesizing life on Earth.

ATP

Certain enzymes catalyze the breakdown of organic foodstuffs. Once sugars are transported into cells, they either serve as building blocks in the form of amino acids for proteins and fatty acids for lipids or are subjected to metabolic pathways to provide the cell with ATP. The common carrier of energy inside the cell, ATP is made from adenosine diphosphate (ADP) and inorganic phosphate (P_i). Stored in the chemical bond holding the terminal phosphate compound onto the ATP molecule is the energy derived from the breakdown of sugars. The removal of the terminal phosphate, through the water-mediated reaction called hydrolysis, releases this energy, which in turn fuels a large number of crucial energy-absorbing reactions in the cell. Hydrolysis can be summarized as follows:

$$ATP + H_2O \rightarrow ADP + P_i + energy$$

The formation of ATP is the reverse of this equation, requiring the addition of energy. The central cellular pathway of ATP synthesis begins with glycolysis, a form of fermentation in which the sugar glucose is transformed into other sugars in a series of nine enzymatic reacwtions, each successive reaction involving an intermediate sugar containing phosphate. In the process, the six-carbon glucose is converted into two molecules of the three carbon pyruvic acid. Some of the energy released through glycolysis of each glucose molecule is captured in the formation of two ATP molecules.

The second stage in the metabolism of sugars is a set of interrelated reactions called the tricarboxylic acid cycle. This cycle takes the three-carbon pyruvic acid produced in glycolysis and uses its carbon atoms to form carbon dioxide (CO_2) while transferring its hydrogen atoms to special carrier molecules, where they are held in high-energy linkage.

In the third and last stage in the breakdown of sugars, oxidative phosphorylation, the high-energy hydrogen atoms are first separated into protons and high-energy electrons. The electrons are then passed from one electron carrier to another by means of an electron-transport chain. Each electron carrier in the chain has an increasing affinity for electrons, with the final electron acceptor being molecular oxygen (O_2). As separated electrons and protons, the hydrogen atoms are transferred to O_2 to form water. This reaction releases a large amount of energy, which drives the synthesis of a large number of ATP molecules from ADP and P_i.

Most of the cell's ATP is produced when the products of glycolysis are oxidized completely by a combination of the tricarboxylic acid cycle and oxidative phosphorylation. The process of glycolysis alone produces relatively small amounts of ATP. Glycolysis is an anaerobic reaction, meaning that it can occur even in the absence of oxygen. Conversely, the tricarboxylic acid cycle and oxidative phosphorylation require oxygen. Glycolysis forms the basis of anaerobic fermentation, and it presumably was a major source of ATP for early life on Earth, when very little oxygen was available in the atmosphere. Eventually, however, bacteria evolved that were able to carry out photosynthesis. Photosynthesis liberated these bacteria from a dependence on the metabolism of organic materials that had accumulated from natural processes, and it also released oxygen into the atmosphere. Over a prolonged period of time, the concentration of molecular oxygen increased until it became freely available in the atmosphere. The aerobic tricarboxylic acid cycle and oxidative phosphorylation then evolved, and the resulting aerobic cells made much more efficient use of foodstuffs than their anaerobic ancestors, because they could convert much larger amounts of chemical bond energy into ATP.

GENETIC INFORMATION

Cells can thus be seen as a self-replicating network of catalytic macromolecules engaged in a carefully balanced series of energy conversions that drive biosynthesis and cell movement. But energy alone is not enough to make self-reproduction possible. The cell must contain detailed instructions that dictate exactly how that energy is to be used. These instructions are analogous to the blueprints that a builder uses to construct a house. In the case of cells, however, the blueprints themselves must be duplicated along with the cell before it divides, so that each daughter cell can retain the instructions that it needs for its own replication. These instructions constitute the cell's heredity.

DNA

During the early 19th century, it became widely accepted that all living organisms are composed of cells arising only from the growth and division of other cells. The improvement of the microscope then led to an era during which many biologists made intensive observations of the microscopic structure of cells. By 1885 a substantial amount of indirect evidence indicated that chromosomes— dark-staining threads in the cell nucleus—carried the information for cell heredity. It was later shown

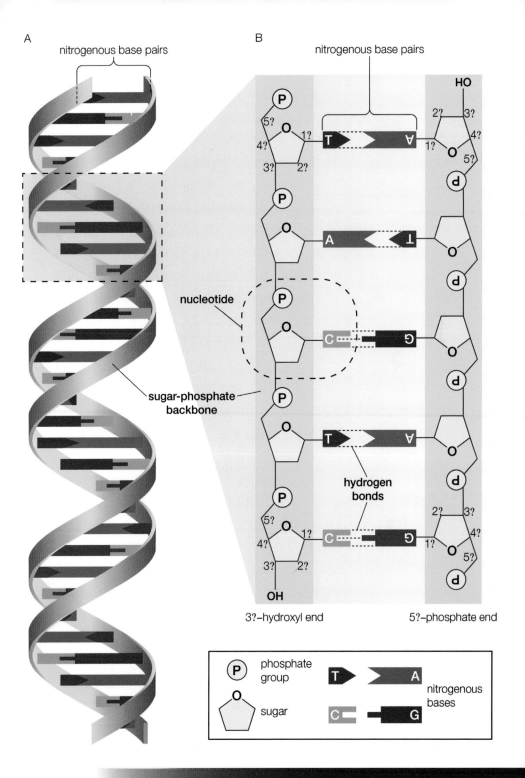

A

nitrogenous base pairs

B

nitrogenous base pairs

HO

P
5?
O
4?   1?
3?   2?
T ▶ ▷ A
2?   3?
4?
1? O
5?
d

P
O
A ◀ ◁ T
O
d

nucleotide

P
O
C ▭ ◼ G
O
d

sugar-phosphate
backbone

P
O
T ▶ ▷ A
O

hydrogen
bonds

d

P
5?
O
4?   1?
3?   2?
C ▭ ◼ G
2?   3?
4?
1? O
5?
d

OH

3?–hydroxyl end   5?–phosphate end

| P | phosphate group | T ▶ ▷ A | nitrogenous bases |
| O | sugar | C ▭ ◼ G | |

This diagram of a DNA molecule shows the base pairs and the double helix structure.

that chromosomes are about half DNA and half protein by weight. The revolutionary discovery suggesting that DNA molecules could provide the information for their own replication came in 1953, when American geneticist and biophysicist James Watson and British biophysicist Francis Crick proposed a model for the structure of the double-stranded DNA molecule (called the DNA double helix). In this model, each strand serves as a template in the synthesis of a complementary strand. Subsequent research confirmed the Watson and Crick model of DNA replication and showed that DNA carries the genetic information for reproduction of the entire cell.

All the genetic information in a cell was initially thought to be confined to the DNA in the chromosomes of the cell nucleus. Later discoveries identified small amounts of additional genetic information present in the DNA of much smaller chromosomes located in two types of organelles in the cytoplasm. These organelles are the mitochondria in animal cells and the mitochondria and chloroplasts in plant cells. The special chromosomes carry the information coding for a few of the many proteins and RNA molecules needed by the organelles. They also hint at the evolutionary origin of these organelles, which are thought to have originated as free-living bacteria that were taken up by other organisms in the process of symbiosis.

RNA

It is possible for RNA to replicate itself by mechanisms related to those used by DNA, even though it has a single-stranded instead of a double-stranded structure. In early cells RNA is thought to have replicated itself in this way. However, all the RNA in present-day cells is synthesized by special enzymes that construct a single-stranded RNA chain by using one strand of the DNA helix as a template. Although RNA molecules are synthesized in the cell nucleus, where the DNA is located, most are transported to the cytoplasm before they carry out their functions.

The RNA molecules in cells have two main roles. Some, the ribozymes, fold up in ways that allow them to serve as catalysts for specific chemical reactions. Others serve as "messenger RNA," which provides templates specifying the synthesis of proteins. Ribosomes, tiny protein-synthesizing machines located in the cytoplasm, "read" the messenger RNA molecules and "translate" them into proteins by using the genetic code. In this translation, the sequence of nucleotides in the messenger RNA chain is decoded three nucleotides at a time, and each nucleotide triplet (called a codon) specifies a particular amino acid. Thus, a nucleotide sequence in the DNA specifies a protein, provided that a messenger RNA molecule is produced from that DNA sequence. Each region of

How DNA directs protein synthesis

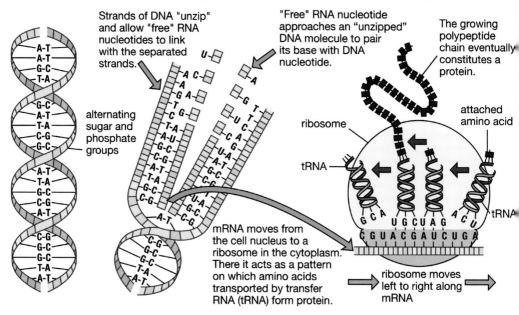

1. Double-stranded DNA in the cell nucleus

2. Messenger RNA (mRNA) forming on DNA strands

3. Formation of protein on ribosome

Strands of DNA "unzip" and allow "free" RNA nucleotides to link with the separated strands.

alternating sugar and phosphate groups

"Free" RNA nucleotide approaches an "unzipped" DNA molecule to pair its base with DNA nucleotide.

The growing polypeptide chain eventually constitutes a protein.

ribosome

tRNA

attached amino acid

mRNA moves from the cell nucleus to a ribosome in the cytoplasm. There it acts as a pattern on which amino acids transported by transfer RNA (tRNA) form protein.

ribosome moves left to right along mRNA

tRNA

Molecular genetics emerged from the realization that DNA and RNA constitute the genetic material of all living organisms. (1) DNA, located in the cell nucleus, is made up of nucleotides that contain the bases adenine (A), thymine (T), guanine (G), and cytosine (C). (2) RNA, which contains uracil (U) instead of thymine, transports the genetic code to protein-synthesizing sites in the cell. (3) Messenger RNA (mRNA) then carries the genetic information to ribosomes in the cell cytoplasm that translate the genetic information into molecules of protein.

the DNA sequence specifying a protein in this way is called a gene.

By the aforementioned mechanisms, DNA molecules catalyze not only their own duplication but also dictate the structures of all protein molecules. A single human cell contains about 10,000 different proteins produced by the expression of 10,000 different genes. Actually, a set of human chromosomes is thought to contain DNA with enough information to express between 30,000 and 100,000 proteins, but most of these proteins seem to be made only in specialized types of cells and are therefore not present throughout the body.

CELLS AND TISSUES

In multicellular organisms, cells are organized into tissues. These organizations consist of structurally and functionally similar cells and of intercellular material. By definition, tissues are absent from unicellular organisms. Even among the simplest multicellular species, such as sponges, tissues are lacking or are poorly differentiated. But multicellular animals and plants that are more advanced have specialized tissues that can organize and regulate an organism's response to its environment.

ANIMAL TISSUES

Early in the evolutionary history of animals, tissues became aggregated into organs, which themselves became divided into specialized parts. An early scientific classification of tissues divided them on the basis of the organ system of which they formed a part (e.g., nervous tissues). Embryologists have often classified tissues on the basis of their origin in the developing embryo, such as ectodermal, endo-dermal, and mesodermal tissues. Another method classified tissues into four broad groups—epithelial, endothelial, stroma, and connective—according to cell composition. In this classification, epithelial tis-sues are composed of cells that make up the body's outer covering and the membranous covering of internal organs, cavities, and canals, and endothelial tissues are composed of cells that line the inside of organs. Stroma tissues are composed of cells that serve as a matrix in which the other cells are embed-ded, whereas connective tissues represent a rather amorphous category composed of cells and an extracellular matrix that serve as a connection from one tissue to another.

The most useful of all systems, however, breaks down animal tissues into four classes based on the functions that the tissues perform. These four tis-sue classes are epithelial tissue, connective tissue, nervous tissue, and muscle tissue. According to this system, epithelial tissues include the layers of cells closely bound to one another that form con-tinuous sheets covering body surfaces internally and externally. Thus, epithelial tissues are those tissues that may come into contact with foreign substances. Connective tissues are groups of cells that maintain the form of the body and its organs and that provide cohesion and internal support. The connective tissues include several types of fibrous tissue that vary only in their density and cellularity, as well as the more specialized and recognizable variants—bone, ligaments, tendons, cartilage, and adipose (fat) tissue.

Nervous tissue consists of organized groups of cells that are specialized for the conduction of electrochemical stimuli. Within nervous tissue, neurons conduct electrical impulses that carry various types of information, and support cells (e.g., neuroglia) exert control on the neuronal environment. Muscle tissue is primarily responsible for movement and consists of contractile cells. There are two general types of muscle: striated muscle, which moves the skeleton and is under voluntary control, and smooth muscle, which surrounds the walls of many internal organs and cannot normally be controlled voluntarily.

The differences between tissue types in animals provide important information about the organisms' evolutionary histories. In addition, the mechanisms that contribute to human health and disease states often can be explained by cellular influences within tissues. Although each tissue specializes in certain functions, the tissues are not isolated from one another. Rather, they are highly integrated, with their full capacity of functions realized only through the maintenance of their interdependencies.

PLANT TISSUES

The ways in which cells are organized into tissues in plants differ fundamentally from the ways in which they are organized into tissues in animals. Vascular plants possess specialized conducting tissues, which transport nutrients and water to all parts of the plant. In contrast, nonvascular plants, such as bryophytes (liverworts, hornworts, and mosses), lack these tissues. Bryophytes further lack true leaves, stems, and roots. As a result, these plants absorb water and nutrients directly through leaflike and stem like structures or through cells that form during certain phases of the reproductive cycle.

In vascular plants, such as angiosperms and gymnosperms, cell division takes place almost exclusively in specific tissues known as meristems. Apical meristems, which are located at the tips of shoots and roots in all vascular plants, give rise to three types of primary meristems, which in turn produce the mature primary tissues of the plant. The three kinds of mature tissues are dermal, vascular, and ground tissues. Primary dermal tissues, called epidermis, make up the outer layer of all plant organs (e.g., stems, roots, leaves, flowers). They help deter excess water loss and invasion by insects and microorganisms. The vascular tissues are of two kinds: water-transporting xylem and food-transporting phloem. Primary xylem and phloem are arranged in vascular bundles that run the length of the plant from roots to leaves. The ground tissues, which comprise the remaining plant matter, include various support, storage, and photosynthetic tissues.

Secondary, or lateral, meristems, which are found in all woody plants and in some herbaceous ones, consist of the vascular cambium and the cork cambium. They produce secondary tissues from a ring of vascular cambium in stems and roots. Secondary phloem forms along the outer edge of the cambium ring, and secondary xylem (i.e., wood) forms along the inner edge of the cambium ring. The cork cambium produces a secondary dermal tissue (periderm) that replaces the epidermis along older stems and roots.

CELL EVOLUTION

The processes underlying the origin and evolution of the first cells on Earth remain a subject of speculation. This is largely because there exists only very limited information concerning early Earth and the conditions that triggered the chemical reactions leading to the eventual generation of cells. Despite this setback, scientists have been able to identify several major evolutionary processes that must have occurred in order to produce the eukaryotic and prokaryotic cells that exist today. Much of this information has come from enlightening laboratory-based studies of cells and genetic material. Two of the most important and extensively studied cellular evolutionary processes are the development of genetic information, which enabled cells to become highly specialized, and the development of metabolism, which gave cells the ability to generate their own energy.

DEVELOPMENT OF DNA AND RNA

Life on Earth could not exist until a collection of catalysts appeared that could promote the synthesis of more catalysts of the same kind. Early stages in the evolutionary pathway of cells presumably centred on RNA molecules, which not only present specific catalytic surfaces but also contain the potential for their own duplication through the formation of a complementary RNA molecule. It is assumed that a small RNA molecule eventually appeared that was able to catalyze its own duplication.

Imperfections in primitive RNA replication likely gave rise to many variant autocatalytic RNA molecules. Molecules of RNA that acquired variations that increased the speed or the fidelity of self-replication would have outmultiplied other, less competent RNA molecules. In addition, other small RNA molecules that existed in symbiosis with autocatalytic RNA molecules underwent natural selection for their ability to catalyze useful secondary reactions such as the production of better precursor molecules. In this way, sophisticated families of RNA catalysts could have evolved together, because cooperation between different molecules produced a system that was much more effective at self-replication than a collection of individual RNA catalysts.

Another major step in the evolution of the cell would have been the development, in one family of self-replicating RNA, of a primitive mechanism of protein synthesis. Protein molecules cannot provide the information for the synthesis of other protein molecules like themselves. This information must ultimately be derived from a nucleic acid sequence. Protein synthesis is much more complex than RNA synthesis, and it could not have arisen before a group of powerful RNA catalysts evolved. Each of these catalysts presumably has its counterpart among the RNA molecules that function in the current cell: (1) there was an information RNA molecule, much like messenger RNA (mRNA), whose nucleotide sequence was read to create an amino acid sequence; (2) there was a group of adaptor RNA molecules, much like transfer RNA (tRNA), that could bind to both mRNA and a specific activated amino acid; and (3) finally, there was an RNA catalyst, much like ribosomal RNA (rRNA), that facilitated the joining together of the amino acids aligned on the mRNA by the adaptor RNA.

At some point in the evolution of biological catalysts, the first cell was formed. This would have required the partitioning of the primitive biological catalysts into individual units, each surrounded by a membrane. Membrane formation might have occurred quite simply, because many amphiphilic molecules— half hydrophobic (water-repelling) and half hydrophilic (water-loving)—aggregate to form bilayer sheets in which the hydrophobic portions of the molecules line up in rows to form the interior of the sheet and leave the hydrophilic portions to face the water. Such bilayer sheets can spontaneously close up to form the walls of small, spherical vesicles, as can the phospholipid bilayer membranes of present-day cells.

As soon as the biological catalysts became compartmentalized into small individual units, or cells, the units would have begun to compete with one another for the same resources. The active competition that ensued must have greatly accelerated evolutionary change, serving as a powerful force for the development of more efficient cells. In this way, cells eventually arose that contained new catalysts, enabling them to use simpler, more abundant precursor molecules for their growth. Because these cells were no longer dependent on preformed ingredients for their survival, they were able to spread far beyond the limited environments where the first primitive cells arose.

It is often assumed that the first cells appeared only after the development of a primitive form of protein synthesis. However, it is by no means certain that cells cannot exist without proteins, and it has been suggested that the first cells contained only RNA catalysts. In either case, protein molecules, with their chemically varied side chains, are more powerful catalysts than RNA molecules. Therefore, as time passed, cells arose in which RNA served primarily as genetic material, being directly replicated in each generation and inherited by all progeny cells in order to specify proteins.

As cells became more complex, a need would have arisen for a stabler form of genetic information storage than that provided by RNA. DNA, related to RNA yet chemically stabler, probably appeared rather late in the evolutionary history of cells. Over a period of time, the genetic information in RNA sequences was transferred to DNA sequences, and the ability of RNA molecules to replicate directly was lost. It was only at this point that the central process of biology—the synthesis, one after the other, of DNA, RNA, and protein—appeared.

DEVELOPMENT OF METABOLISM

The first cells presumably resembled prokaryotic cells in lacking nuclei and functional internal compartments, or organelles. These early cells were also anaerobic (not requiring oxygen), deriving their energy from the fermentation of organic molecules that had previously accumulated on Earth over long periods of time.

Eventually, more sophisticated cells evolved that could carry out primitive forms of photosynthesis, in which light energy was harnessed by membrane-bound proteins to form organic molecules with energy-rich chemical bonds. A major turning point in the evolution of life was the development of photosynthesizing prokaryotes requiring only water as an electron donor and capable of producing molecular oxygen. The descendants of these prokaryotes, the blue-green algae (cyanobacteria), still exist as viable life-forms. Their ancestors prospered to such an extent that the atmosphere became rich in the oxygen they produced. The free availability of this oxygen in turn enabled other prokaryotes to evolve aerobic forms of metabolism that were much more efficient in the use of organic molecules as a source of food.

The switch to predominantly aerobic metabolism is thought to have occurred in bacteria approximately 2 billion years ago, about 1.5 billion to 1.8 billion years after the first cells had formed. Aerobic eukaryotic cells probably appeared about 1.5 billion years ago, their lineage having branched off much earlier from that of the prokaryotes. Eukaryotic cells almost certainly became aerobic by engulfing aerobic prokaryotes, with which they lived in a symbiotic relationship. The mitochondria found in both animals and plants are the descendants of such prokaryotes. Later, in branches of the eukaryotic lineage leading to plants and algae, a blue-green algaelike organism was engulfed to perform photosynthesis. It is likely that over a long period of time these organisms became the chloroplasts.

The eukaryotic cell thus apparently arose as an amalgam of different cells, in the process becoming an efficient aerobic cell whose plasma membrane was freed from energy metabolism—one of the major functions of the cell membrane of prokaryotes. The eukaryotic cell membrane was therefore able to become specialized for cell-to-cell communication and cell signaling. It may be partly for this reason that eukaryotic cells were eventually more successful at forming complex multicellular organisms than their simpler prokaryotic relatives.

DEVELOPMENT OF MITOCHONDRIA AND CHLOROPLASTS

In addition to their remarkable metabolic capabilities, both mitochondria and chloroplasts synthesize on their own a number of proteins and lipids necessary for their structure and activity. Not only do they contain the machinery necessary for this, but they also possess the genetic material to direct it. DNA within these organelles has a circular structure reminiscent of prokaryotic, not eukaryotic, DNA. Also as in prokaryotes, the DNA is not associated with histones. Along with the DNA are protein-synthesizing ribosomes, of prokaryotic rather than eukaryotic size.

Only a small portion of the mitochondrion's total number of proteins is synthesized within the organelle. Numerous proteins are encoded and made in the cytoplasm specifically for export into the mitochondrion. The mitochondrial DNA itself encodes only 13 different proteins. The proteins that contain subunits synthesized within the mitochondrion often also possess subunits synthesized in the cytoplasm. Mitochondrial and chloroplastic proteins synthesized in the cytoplasm have to enter the organelle by a complex process, crossing both the outer and the inner membranes. These proteins contain specific arrangements of amino acids known as leader sequences that are recognized by receptors on the outer membranes of the organelles. The proteins are then guided through membrane channels in an energy-requiring process.

Mitochondria and chloroplasts are self-dividing. They contain their own DNA and protein-synthesizing machinery, similar to that of prokaryotes. Chloroplasts produce ATP and trap photons by mechanisms that are complex and yet similar to those of certain pro-karyotes. These phenomena have led to the theory that the two organelles are direct descendants of prokaryotes that entered primitive nucleated cells. Among billions of such events, a few could have led to the development of stable, symbiotic associations between nucleated hosts and prokaryotic parasites. The hosts would provide the parasites with a stable osmotic environment and easy access to nutrients, and the parasites would repay the hosts by providing an oxidative ATP-producing system or a photosyn-thetic energy-producing reaction.

CELL MEMBRANES AND CELL WALLS

The contents of all cells are enveloped by a highly specialized cell membrane. This membrane is a chemically complex structure and consists of multiple components, each of which contributes to the unique functions performed by the membrane. One of the most important of these functions is to serve as a protective layer, defending the cell interior against physical insult. In plants, a rigid cell wall reinforces this function, endowing stems, leaves, and roots with exceptional strength in the face of physical challenges ranging from wind to rain to sunlight. Prokaryotes also have cell walls, as do the cells of fungi and some algae.

Contrasted against this physical role is the intricate regulatory nature of the membrane, which influences a variety of cellular activities, including the uptake of nutrients, cell-to-cell adhesion, and cell communication. There are diverse arrays of receptors and channels that recognize specific types of molecules, allowing them to enter and leave cells only under certain conditions, which are dictated by both intracellular and extracellular factors. This regulatory ability is one of the most complex and amazing features of cell membranes.

CELL MEMBRANE STRUCTURE

A thin membrane surrounds every living cell, delimiting the cell from the environment around it. Enclosed by this cell membrane (also known as the plasma membrane) are the cell's constituents, often large, water-soluble, highly charged molecules such as proteins, nucleic acids, carbohydrates, and substances involved in cellular metabolism. Outside the cell, in the surrounding water-based environment, are ions, acids, and alkalis that are toxic to the cell, as well as nutrients that the cell must absorb in order to live and grow. The cell membrane, therefore, has two functions: first, to be a barrier keeping the constituents of the cell in and unwanted substances out and, second, to be a gate allowing transport into the cell of essential nutrients and movement from the cell of waste products.

Most current knowledge about the biochemical constituents of cell membranes originates in studies of red blood cells. The chief advantage of

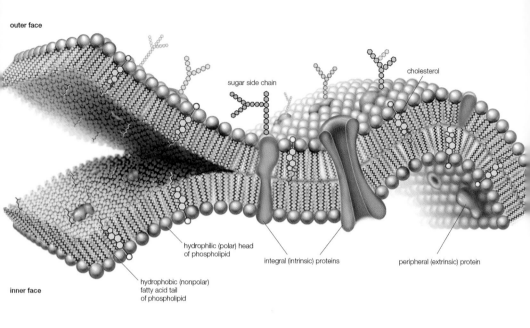

outer face

sugar side chain

cholesterol

hydrophilic (polar) head
of phospholipid

integral (intrinsic) proteins

peripheral (extrinsic) protein

inner face

hydrophobic (nonpolar)
fatty acid tail
of phospholipid

Intrinsic proteins penetrate and bind tightly to the lipid bilayer, which is made up largely of phospholipids and cholesterol and which typically is between 4 and 10 nanometers (nm; 1 nm = 10 metre) in thickness. Extrinsic proteins are loosely bound to the hydrophilic (polar) surfaces, which face the watery medium both inside and outside the cell. Some intrinsic proteins present sugar side chains on the cell's outer surface.

these cells for experimental purposes is that they may be obtained easily in large amounts and that they have no internal membranous organelles to interfere with study of their cell membranes. Careful studies of these and other cell types have shown that all membranes are composed of proteins and fatty-acid-based lipids. Membranes actively involved in metabolism contain a higher proportion of protein. Thus, the membrane of the mitochondrion, the most rapidly metabolizing organelle of the cell, contains as much as 75 percent protein, while the membrane of the Schwann cell, which forms an insulating sheath around many nerve cells, has as little as 20 percent protein.

LIPIDS

Membrane lipids are principally of two types, phospholipids and sterols (generally cholesterol). Both types share the defining characteristic of lipids—they dissolve readily in organic solvents—but in addition they both have a region that is attracted to and soluble in water. This "amphiphilic" property (having a dual attraction; i.e., containing both a lipid-soluble and a water-soluble region) is basic to the role of lipids as building blocks of cellular membranes. Phospholipid molecules have a head (often of glycerol) to which are attached two long fatty acid chains that look much like tails. These tails are repelled by water and dissolve readily in organic solvents, giving the molecule its lipid character. To another part of the head is attached a phosphoryl group with a negative electrical charge, and to this group in turn is attached another group with a positive or neutral charge. This portion of the phospholipid dissolves in water, thereby completing the molecule's amphiphilic character. In contrast, sterols have a complex hydrocarbon ring structure as the lipid-soluble region and a hydroxyl grouping as the water-soluble region.

When dry phospholipids, or a mixture of such phospholipids and cholesterol, are immersed in water under laboratory conditions, they spontaneously form globular structures called liposomes. Investigation of the liposomes shows them to be made of concentric spheres, one sphere inside of another and each forming half of a bilayered wall. A bilayer is composed of two sheets of phospholipid molecules with all of the molecules of each sheet aligned in the same direction. In a water medium, the phospholipids of the two sheets align so that their water-repellent, lipid-soluble tails are turned and loosely bonded to the tails of the molecules on the other sheet. The water-soluble heads turn outward into the water, to which they are chemically attracted. In this way, the two sheets form a fluid, sandwichlike structure, with the fatty acid chains in the middle mingling in an organic medium while sealing out the water medium.

This type of lipid bilayer, formed by the self-assembly of lipid molecules, is the basic structure of the cell membrane. It is the most stable thermodynamic structure that a phospholipid-water mixture can take up: the fatty acid portion of each molecule dissolved in the organic phase formed by the identical regions of the other molecules and the water-attractive regions surrounded by water and facing away from the fatty acid regions. The chemical affinity of each region of the amphiphilic molecule is thus satisfied in the bilayer structure.

PROTEINS

Membrane proteins are also of two general types. One type, called the extrinsic proteins, is loosely attached by ionic bonds or calcium bridges to the electrically charged phosphoryl surface of the bilayer. They can also attach to the second type of protein, called the intrinsic proteins. The intrinsic proteins, as their name implies, are firmly embedded within the phospholipid bilayer. Almost all intrinsic proteins contain special amino acid sequences, generally about 20 to 24 amino acids long, that extend through the internal regions of the cell membrane.

Most intrinsic and extrinsic proteins bear on their outer surfaces side chains of complex sugars, which extend into the aqueous environment around the cell. For this reason, these proteins are often referred to as glycoproteins. Some glycoproteins are involved in cell-to-cell recognition.

FLUIDITY

One of the triumphs of cell biology during the decade from 1965 to 1975 was the recognition of the cell membrane as a fluid collection of amphiphilic molecules. This array of proteins, sterols, and phospholipids is organized into a liquid crystal, a structure that lends itself readily to rapid cell growth. Measurements of the membrane's viscosity show it as a fluid one hundred times as viscous as water, similar to a thin oil. The phospholipid molecules diffuse readily in the plane of the bilayer. Many of the membrane's proteins also have this freedom of movement, but some are fixed in the membrane by interaction with the cell's cytoskeleton. Newly synthesized phospholipids insert themselves easily into the existing cell membrane. Intrinsic proteins are inserted during their synthesis on ribosomes bound to the endoplasmic reticulum, whereas extrinsic proteins found on the internal surface of the cell membrane are synthesized on free, or unattached, ribosomes, liberated into the cytoplasm, and then brought to the membrane.

CELL MEMBRANE TRANSPORT

The chemical structure of the cell membrane makes it remarkably flexible, the ideal boundary for rapidly growing and dividing cells. Yet the membrane is also a formidable barrier, allowing some dissolved substances, or solutes, to pass while blocking others. Lipid-soluble molecules and some small molecules can permeate the membrane, but the lipid bilayer

effectively repels the many large water-soluble molecules and electrically charged ions that the cell
must import or export to live. Transport of these vital
substances is carried out by certain classes of intrinsic proteins that form a variety of transport systems:
some are open channels, which allow ions to diffuse
directly into the cell; others are "facilitators," which,
through a little-understood chemical transformation,
help solutes diffuse past the lipid screen; yet others
are "pumps," which force solutes through the membrane when they are not concentrated enough to
diffuse spontaneously. Particles too large to be dif-
fused or pumped are often swallowed or disgorged
whole by an opening and closing of the membrane.

Behind this movement of solutes across the cell
membrane is the principle of diffusion. According to
this principle, a dissolved substance diffuses down
a concentration gradient. In other words, given no
energy from an outside source, it moves from a place
where its concentration is high to a place where its
concentration is low. Diffusion continues down this
gradually decreasing gradient until a state of equilibrium is reached, at which point there is an equal
concentration in both places and an equal, random
diffusion in both directions.

A solute at high concentration is at high free
energy, meaning that it is capable of doing more
"work" (the work being that of diffusion) than a solute at low concentration. In performing the work of

diffusion, the solute loses free energy, so that, when it reaches equilibrium at a lower concentration, it is unable to return spontaneously (under its own energy) to its former high concentration. However, by the addition of energy from an outside source (through the work of an ion pump, for example), the solute may be returned to its former concentration and state of high free energy. This "coupling" of work processes is, in effect, a transferal of free energy from the pump to the solute, which is then able to repeat the work of diffusion.

For most substances of biological interest, the concentrations inside and outside the cell are different, creating concentration gradients down which the solutes spontaneously diffuse, provided they can permeate the lipid bilayer. Membrane channels and diffusion facilitators bring them through the membrane by passive transport. Thus, the changes that the proteins undergo to facilitate diffusion are powered by the diffusing solutes themselves. For the healthy functioning of the cell, certain solutes must remain at different concentrations on each side of the membrane. If through diffusion they approach equilibrium, they must be pumped back up their gradients by the process of active transport. Those membrane proteins serving as pumps accomplish this by coupling the energy required for transport to the energy produced by cell metabolism or by the diffusion of other solutes.

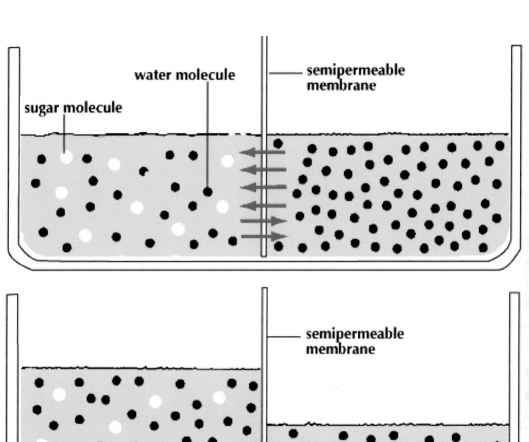

The principle of permeation can be illustrated by differences in the diffusion of sugar and water through a membrane. Large sugar molecules in the solution cannot pass through the membrane into the water (*top*). In contrast, small water molecules easily diffuse through the membrane (*bottom*). The ability of water to readily cross membranes is vital for establishing equilibrium.

PERMEATION

Permeation is the diffusion, through a barrier, of a substance in solution. The rates at which biologically important molecules cross the cell membrane through permeation vary over an enormous range. Proteins and sugar polymers do not permeate at all. In contrast, water and alcohols permeate most membranes in less than a second. This variation, caused by the lipid bilayer, gives the membrane its characteristic permeability. Permeability is measured as the rate at which a particular substance in solution crosses the membrane.

For all cell membranes that have been studied in the laboratory, permeability increases in parallel with the permeant's ability to dissolve in organic solvents. The consistency of this parallel has led researchers to conclude that permeability is a function of the fatty acid interior of the lipid bilayer, rather than its phosphoryl exterior. This property of dissolving in organic solvents rather than water is given a unit of measure called the partition coefficient. The greater the solubility of a substance, the higher its partition coefficient, and the higher the partition coefficient, the higher the permeability of the membrane to that particular substance. For example, the water solubility of hydroxyl, carboxyl, and amino groups reduces their solubility in organic solvents and, hence, their partition coefficients. Cell membranes have been observed to have low permeability toward these groups. In contrast, lipidsoluble methyl residues and hydrocarbon rings, which have high partition coefficients, penetrate cell membranes more easily—a property useful in designing chemotherapeutic and pharmacological drugs.

For two molecules of the same partition coefficient, the one of greater molecular weight, or size, will in general cross the membrane more slowly. In fact, even molecules with very low partition coefficients can penetrate the membrane if they are small enough. Water, for example, is insoluble in organic solvents, yet it permeates cell membranes because of the small size of its molecules. The size selectivity of the lipid bilayer is a result of its being not a simple fluid, the molecules of which move around and past a diffusing molecule, but an organized matrix, a kind of fixed grate, composed of the fatty acid chains of the phospholipids through which the diffusing molecule must fit.

Many substances do not actually cross the cell membrane through permeation of the lipid bilayer. Some electrically charged ions, for example, are repelled by organic solvents and therefore cross cell membranes with great difficulty, if at all. In these cases special holes in the membrane, called channels, allow specific ions and small molecules to diffuse directly through the bilayer.

MEMBRANE CHANNELS

Biophysicists measuring the electric current passing through cell membranes have found that, in general, cell membranes have a vastly greater electrical conductance than does a membrane bilayer composed only of phospholipids and sterols. This greater conductance is thought to be conferred by the cell membrane's proteins. A current flowing across a membrane often appears on a recording instrument as a series of bursts of various heights. These bursts represent current flowing through open channels, which are merely holes formed by intrinsic proteins traversing the lipid bilayer. No significant current flows through the membrane when no channel is open. Multiple bursts are recorded when more than one channel is open.

A rich variety of channels has been isolated and analyzed from a wide range of cell membranes. Invariably intrinsic proteins, they contain numerous amino acid sequences that traverse the membrane, clearly forming a specific hole, or pore. Certain channels open and close spontaneously. Some are gated, or opened, by the chemical action of a signaling substance such as calcium, acetylcholine, or glycine, whereas others are gated by changes in the electrical potential across the membrane. Channels may possess a narrow specificity, allowing passage of only potassium or sodium, or a broad specificity, allowing

A

concentration gradient

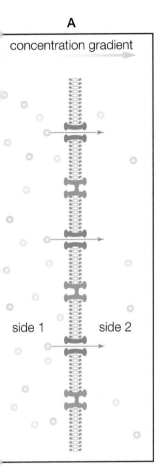

side 1   side 2

B

concentration gradient
electrostatic force

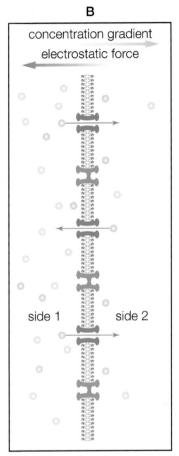

side 1   side 2

C

equilibrium potential

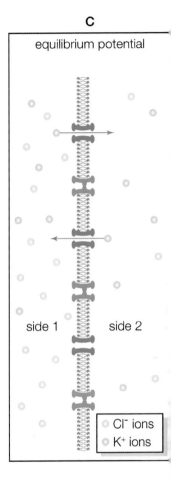

side 1   side 2

○ Cl⁻ ions
○ K⁺ ions

(A) A high concentration of KCl is placed on side 1, opposite a semipermeable membrane from a low concentration. The membrane allows only K to diffuse, thereby establishing an electrical potential difference across the membrane. (B) The separation of charge creates an electrostatic voltage force, which draws some K back to side 1. (C) At equilibrium, there is no net flux of K in either direction. Side 1, with the higher concentration of KCl, has a negative charge compared with side 2.

passage of all positively charged ions (cations) or of all negatively charged ions (anions). There are channels called gap junctions that allow the passage of molecules between pairs of cells.

The gating of channels with a capacity for ion transport is the basis of the many nerve-nerve, nerve-muscle, and nerve-gland interactions underlying neurobiological behaviour. These actions depend on the electric potential of the cell membrane, which varies with the prevailing constituents in the cell's environment. For example, if a channel that admits only potassium ions is present in a membrane separating two different potassium chloride solutions, the positively charged potassium ions tend to flow down their concentration gradient through the channel. The negatively charged chloride ions remain behind. This separation of electric charges sets up an electric potential across the membrane called the diffusion potential. The size of this potential depends on, among other factors, the difference in concentrations of the permeating ion across the membrane. The cell membrane in general contains the channels of widely different ion specificities, each channel contributing to the overall membrane potential according to the permeability and concentration ratio of the ion passing through it. Because the channels are often gated, the membrane's potential is determined by which channels are open. This in turn depends on the concentrations of signaling molecules and may change with time according to the membrane potential itself.

Most cells have about a tenfold higher concentration of sodium ions outside than inside and a reverse concentration ratio of potassium ions. Free calcium ions can be 10,000 times more concentrated outside the cell than inside. Thus, sodium-, potassium-, and calcium-selective membrane channels, by allowing the diffusion of those ions past the cell membrane and causing fluctuations in the membrane's electric potential, frequently serve as transmitters of signals from nerve cells. Ion diffusion threatens to alter the concentration of ions necessary for the cell to function. The proper distribution of ions is restored by the action of ion pumps.

FACILITATED DIFFUSION

Many water-soluble molecules that cannot penetrate the lipid bilayer are too large to fit through open channels. In this category are sugars and amino acids. Some ions, too, do not diffuse through channels. These vital substances enter and leave the cell through the action of membrane transporters, which, like channels, are intrinsic proteins that traverse the cell membrane. Unlike channels, transporter molecules do not simply open holes in the membrane. Rather, they present sites on one side of the membrane to which molecules bind through chemical attraction. The binding site is highly specific, often fitting the atomic structure of only one type of molecule. When the molecule has attached to the binding site, then, in a process not fully understood, the transporter brings it through the membrane and releases it on the other side.

This action is considered a type of diffusion because the transported molecules move down their concentration gradients, from high concentration to low. To activate the action of the transporter, no other energy is needed than that of the chemical binding of the transported molecules. This action upon the transporter is similar to catalysis, except that the molecules (in this context called substrates) catalyze not a chemical reaction but their own translocation across the cell membrane. Two such substrates are glucose and the bicarbonate ion.

The sugar-specific transport system of a cell enables half of the glucose present inside the cell to leave within four seconds at normal body temperature. The glucose transporter is clearly not a simple membrane channel. First, unlike a channel, it does not select its permeants by size, as one type of glucose is observed to move through the system a thousand times faster than its identically sized optical isomer. Second, it operates much more slowly than do most channels, moving only 1,000 molecules per second while a channel moves 1,000,000 ions. The most important difference between a membrane channel

RESEARCH ON VESICLE TRANSPORT

James E. Rothman (1950–), Randy W. Schekman (1948–), and Thomas C. Südhof (1955–) shared the 2013 Nobel Prize for Physiology or Medicine for their work on vesicle transport in cells. Cellular vesicles, which are bubblelike structures, play a critical role in the storage and transport of molecules within cells, and errors in their function can lead to various diseases, including immunological, neurological, and metabolic disorders.

Rothman discovered the molecular machinery involved in vesicle budding and membrane fusion in cells. He earned a bachelor's degree in physics in 1971 from Yale University and a doctorate in biological chemistry in 1976 from Harvard University, where he also studied medicine. In 1978, after conducting postdoctoral research in biology under American scientist Harvey F. Lodish at the Massachusetts Institute of Technology, Rothman took a professorship in biochemistry at Stanford University. He remained there until 1988, after which he served at Princeton University (1988–91) and Memorial Sloan-Kettering Cancer Center in New York (1991–2004). He joined the faculty of Columbia University in 2003/2004 and that of Yale in 2008. At Yale, Rothman was a professor of cell biology and chemistry and director of the Nanobiology Institute.

Rothman began investigating the machinery of vesicle budding and fusion in the late 1970s. He later

(Continued on the next page)

(Continued from the previous page)

conducted his experiments by using a cell-free system, in which the molecules thought to be important in vesicle transport were added to a test tube in an attempt to reconstitute the process and thereby eliminate certain complexities associated with the cellular environment. In the late 1980s and early 1990s, Rothman and colleagues identified a set of molecules—a protein called NSF and a family of proteins known as SNAP—that serve key functions in membrane trafficking. He subsequently discovered that a complex of SNARE proteins was fundamental to vesicle membrane fusion. Rothman's work provided important insight into the role of the Golgi apparatus in protein processing. He later investigated the biophysics and regulation of vesicle fusion and the organization of the Golgi apparatus.

Schekman's work provided insight into the genetic mechanisms underlying vesicle transport. After completing a bachelor's degree in molecular biology at the University of California, Los Angeles, he attended Stanford University, where he performed his graduate research in the laboratory of American biochemist and physician Arthur Kornberg. Schekman earned a doctorate in biochemistry in 1974. After completing his postdoctoral studies, he became an assistant professor at the University of California, Berkeley, where he later received a professorship in molecular and cell biology.

At Berkeley, Schekman began investigating networks of intracellular membranes associated with the vesicle transport of proteins in the yeast *Saccharomyces cerevisiae*. With the aid of others in his laboratory, he screened yeast for mutations that blocked the secretion of certain enzymes from cells. The work led to the discovery of membrane fusion regulator proteins encoded by SEC genes. The regulator encoded by *SEC1* was later found to interact with SNAP. In subsequent work Schekman and colleagues discovered that nearly two dozen genes play a role in vesicle transport. They characterized the function of each gene's protein and elucidated the sequence in which the proteins act to effect transport. Schekman's work also provided insight into mechanisms of vesicle budding and protein transport from the endoplasmic reticulum.

Südhof discovered key molecular components and mechanisms that form the basis of chemical signaling in neurons. His findings helped scientists to better understand the cellular mechanisms underlying neurological conditions such as autism, schizophrenia, and Alzheimer disease. In 1982 he received a medical degree from the University of Göttingen and a doctorate in neurochemistry from the Max Planck Institute for Biophysical Chemistry, where he investigated the release of hormones from cells of the adrenal glands. The following year Südhof began his postdoctoral studies at the University of Texas Southwestern Medical Center at Dallas. There he investigated the low-density lipoprotein (LDL)

(Continued on the next page)

(Continued from the previous page)

receptor, a molecule involved in cholesterol metabolism. His mentors, American molecular geneticists Michael S. Brown and Joseph L. Goldstein, received the Nobel Prize for Physiology or Medicine (1985) for their cholesterol research while Südhof was a student in their laboratory. In 1986 Südhof became an investigator at Texas Southwestern and an investigator with the Howard Hughes Medical Institute. He moved his laboratory to Stanford University in 2008.

Throughout his career much of Südhof's research focused on presynaptic neurons, which release signaling chemicals called neurotransmitters into the synapse (or junction) between communicating cells (i.e., between neurons, between neurons and muscle cells, or between neurons and glands). He elucidated the process by which synaptic vesicles, which are filled with neurotransmitters, fuse with neuronal membranes and undergo exocytosis, in which they release their neurotransmitters into the extracellular environment. He found that specific interactions between proteins, such as between Munc18-1 and SNARE proteins, as well as a molecular complex based on the proteins RIM and Munc13, are required for synaptic vesicle fusion. He also described a process whereby calcium triggers vesicle fusion and exocytosis via binding to synaptic vesicle proteins known as synaptotagmins and identified presynaptic and postsynaptic proteins, called neurexins and neuroligins, respectively, that associate with one another and form a physical connection across the synaptic cleft (the gap found between the two neurons at a synapse). He later investigated mutations in neurexins and neuroligins and their relevance to neurological conditions such as autism.

and the glucose transporter is the conformational change that the transporter undergoes while moving glucose across the membrane. Alternating between two conformations, it moves its glucose-binding site from one side of the membrane to the other. By "flipping" between its two conformational states, the transporter facilitates the diffusion of glucose—enabling glucose to avoid the barrier of the cell membrane while moving spontaneously down its concentration gradient. When the concentration reaches equilibrium, net movement of glucose ceases. A facilitated diffusion system for glucose is present in many cell types. Similar systems transporting a wide range of other substrates (e.g., different sugars, amino acids, nucleosides, and ions) are also present.

The best studied of the facilitated diffusion systems is that which catalyzes the exchange of anions across the red blood cell membrane. The exchange of hydroxyl for bicarbonate ions, each ion simultaneously being moved down its concentration gradient in opposite directions by the same transport molecule, is of great importance in enhancing the blood's capacity to carry carbon dioxide from tissues to the lungs. The exchange molecule for these anions is the major intrinsic protein of red blood cells—one million of them are present on each cell, the polypeptide chain of each molecule traversing the membrane at least six times.

SECONDARY ACTIVE TRANSPORT

In some cases the problem of forcing a substrate up its concentration gradient is solved by coupling that upward movement to the downward flow of another substrate. In this way the energy-expending diffusion of the driving substrate powers the energy-absorbing movement of the driven substrate from low concentration to high. Because this type of active transport is not powered directly by the energy released in cell metabolism, it is called secondary. There are two kinds of secondary active transport: counter-transport, in which the two substrates cross the membrane in opposite directions, and cotransport, in which they cross in the same direction.

COUNTER-TRANSPORT

An example of the counter-transport system (also called antiport) begins with the sugar transporter already described. There are equal concentrations of glucose on both sides of the cell. A high concentration of galactose is then added outside the cell. Galactose competes with glucose for binding sites on the transport protein, so that mostly galactose—and a little glucose—enter the cell. The transporter itself, undergoing a conformational change, presents its binding sites for sugar at the inner face of the membrane. Here, at least transiently, glucose is in excess of galactose. Glucose binds to the transporter and leaves the cell as the transporter switches back to its original conformation. Thus, glucose is pumped out of the cell against its gradient in exchange for the galactose riding into the cell down its own gradient.

Many counter-transport systems operate across the cell membranes of the body. A well-studied system (present in red blood cells, nerve cells, and muscle cells) pumps one calcium ion out of the cell in exchange for two or three sodium ions. This system helps maintain the low calcium concentration required for effective cellular activity. A different system, present in kidney cells, counter-transports hydrogen ions and sodium ions in a one-for-one ratio. This is important in stabilizing acidity by transporting hydrogen ions out of the body as needed.

CO-TRANSPORT

In co-transport (sometimes called symport) two species of substrate, generally an ion and another molecule or ion, must bind simultaneously to the transporter before its conformational change can take place. As the driving substrate is transported down its concentration gradient, it drags with it the driven substrate, which is forced to move up its concentration gradient. The transporter must be able to undergo a conformational change when not bound to either substrate, so as to complete the cycle and return the binding sites to the side from which driving and driven substrates both move.

Sodium ions are usually the driving substrates in the co-transport systems of animal cells, which maintain high concentrations of these ions through primary active transport. The driven substrates include a variety of sugars, amino acids, and other ions. During the absorption of nutrients, for example, sugars and amino acids are removed from the intestine by co-transport with sodium ions. After passing across the glomerular filter in the kidney, these substrates are returned to the body by the same system. Plant and bacterial cells usually use hydrogen ions as the driving substrate. Sugars and amino acids are the most common driven substrates. When the bacterium *Escherichia coli* must metabolize lactose, it co-transports hydrogen ions with lactose (which can reach a concentration 1,000 times higher than that outside the cell).

PRIMARY ACTIVE TRANSPORT

Another type of transport system present in cell membranes is known as primary active transport, which moves charged particles (ions) up their concentration gradients. Primary active transport mediates the movement of ions through the direct use of energy. The majority of primary active transport systems derive energy from adenosine triphosphate, or ATP. Major active transport systems include sodium-potassium pumps, calcium pumps, and hydrogen ion pumps.

THE SODIUM-POTASSIUM PUMP

Human red blood cells contain a high concentration of potassium and a low concentration of sodium, yet the plasma bathing the cells is high in sodium and low in potassium. When whole blood is stored cold under laboratory conditions, the cells lose potassium and gain sodium until the concentrations across the membrane for both ions are at equilibrium. When the cells are restored to body temperature and given appropriate nutrition, they extrude sodium and take up potassium, transporting both ions against their respective gradients until the previous high concentrations are reached. This ion pumping is linked directly to the hydrolysis of ATP, the cell's repository of metabolic energy. For every molecule of ATP split, three ions of sodium are pumped out of the cell and two of potassium are pumped in.

An enzyme called sodium-potassium-activated ATPase (Na$^+$-K$^+$ ATPase) has been shown to be the sodium-potassium pump, the protein that transports the ions across the cell membrane while splitting ATP. Widely distributed in the animal kingdom and always associated with the cell membrane, this ATPase is found at high concentration in cells that pump large amounts of sodium (e.g., in mammalian kidneys, in salt-secreting glands of marine birds, and in the electric organs of eels). The enzyme, an intrinsic protein, exists in two major conformations whose interconversion is driven by the splitting of ATP or by changes in the transmembrane flows of sodium and potassium. When only sodium is present in the cell, the inorganic phosphate split from ATP during hydrolysis is transferred to the enzyme. Release of the chemically bound phosphate from the enzyme is catalyzed by potassium. Thus, the complete action of ATP splitting has been demonstrated to require both sodium (to catalyze the transfer of the phosphate to the enzyme) and potassium (to catalyze the release of the phosphate and free the enzyme for a further cycle of ATP splitting). Apparently, only after sodium has catalyzed the transferal of the phosphate to the enzyme can it be transported from the cell. Similarly, only after potassium has released the phosphate from the enzyme can it be transported

DISCOVERING NA⁺-K⁺ ATPASE

Danish biophysicist Jens Christian Skou (1918–) won the Nobel Prize for Chemistry in 1997 for his discovery of the enzyme called sodium-potassium-activated adenosine triphosphatase (Na^+-K^+ ATPase), which is found in the plasma membrane of animal cells and acts as a pump that exchanges sodium (Na^+) for potassium (K^+). He shared the prize with Paul D. Boyer and John E. Walker, who explained the enzymatic process involved in the production of the energy-carrying molecule ATP.

Skou's research on ion-carrying enzymes was based on the work of Sir Alan Hodgkin and Richard Keynes, who followed the movements of sodium and potassium in a nerve cell following stimulation. The English scientists discovered that upon activation of the neuron, sodium ions flood the cell. The sodium concentration level is restored when ions are transported back across the membrane. This process requires energy, since transport occurs against a concentration gradient (from an area of low concentration to high concentration) and so was believed to require energy in the form of ATP.

In the late 1950s, Skou proposed that an enzyme is responsible for the transport of molecules through a cell's membrane. His work with the membranes of nerve cells from crabs led to the discovery of Na^+-K^+ ATPase. Bound to a cell membrane, Na^+-K^+ ATPase is activated by external potassium and internal sodium. The enzyme pumps sodium out of the cell and potassium into it,

(Continued on the next page)

(Continued from the previous page)
thereby maintaining a high intracellular concentration of potassium and a low concentration of sodium relative to the surrounding external environment. Skou's work led to the discovery of similar ATPase-based enzymes, including the ion pump that controls muscle contraction.

into the cell. This overall reaction, completing the cycle of conformational changes in the enzyme, involves a strict coupling of the splitting of ATP with the pumping of sodium and potassium. It is this coupling that creates primary active transport.

The sodium-potassium pump extrudes one net positive charge during each cycle of ATP splitting. This flow of current induces an electric potential across the membrane that adds to the potentials brought about by the diffusion of ions through gated channels. The pump's contribution to the overall potential is important in certain specialized nerve cells.

Calcium Pumps

Many animal cells can perform a primary active transport of calcium out of the cell, developing a 10,000-fold gradient of that ion. Calcium-activated ATPases have been isolated and shown to be intrinsic proteins straddling the membrane and undergoing conformational changes similar to those of the sodium-potassium-activated ATPase. When a rise in the concentration of cellular calcium results from the opening of calcium-selective channels, the membrane's calcium pumps restore the low concentration.

HYDROGEN ION PUMPS

Hydrochloric acid is produced in the stomach by the active transport of hydrogen ions from the blood across the stomach lining, or gastric mucosa. Hydrogen concentration gradients of nearly one million can be achieved by a hydrogen-potassium-activated ATP-splitting intrinsic protein in the cells lining the stomach. Apart from its specific ion requirements, the properties of this enzyme are remarkably similar to those of the sodium-potassium activated enzyme and the calcium-activated enzyme. Other hydrogen-pumping ATP-splitting primary active transporters occur in intracellular organelles, in bacteria, and in plant cells. The steep gradient of hydrogen ions represents a store of energy that can be harnessed to the accumulation of nutrients or, in the case of bacterial flagella, to the powering of cell movement.

EXOCYTOSIS AND ENDOCYTOSIS

In bringing about transmembrane movements of large molecules, the cell membrane itself undergoes concerted movements during which part of

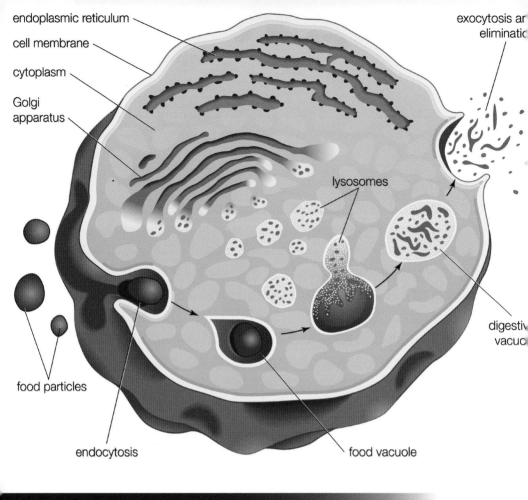

endoplasmic reticulum

cell membrane

cytoplasm

Golgi apparatus

lysosomes

digestiv
vacuc

food particles

endocytosis

food vacuole

Endocytosis and exocytosis are fundamental to the process of intracellular digestion. Food particles are taken into the cell via endocytosis into a vacuole. Lysosomes attach to the vacuole and release digestive enzymes to extract nutrients. The leftover waste products of digestion are carried to the plasma membrane by the vacuole and eliminated through the process of exocytosis.

the fluid medium outside of the cell is internalized (endocytosis) or part of the cell's internal medium is externalized (exocytosis). These movements involve a fusion between membrane surfaces, followed by the re-formation of intact membranes.

In exocytosis, material synthesized within the cell that has been packaged into membrane-bound vesicles is exported from the cell following the fusion of the vesicles with the external cell membrane. The materials exported are cell-specific protein products, neurotransmitters, and a variety of other molecules. In endocytosis, the cell membrane engulfs portions of the external medium, forms an almost complete sphere around it, and then draws the membrane-bounded vesicle, called an endosome, into the cell. Several types of endocytosis have been distinguished: pinocytosis, phagocytosis, and receptor-mediated endocytosis, in which material binds to a specific receptor on the external face of the cell membrane, triggering the process by which it is engulfed. Cholesterol enters cells by the last route.

Pinocytosis is a process by which liquid droplets are ingested by living cells. In pinocytosis, rather than an individual droplet of liquid traveling passively through the cell membrane, the droplet first becomes bound, or adsorbed, on the cell membrane, which then invaginates (forms a pocket) and pinches off to form a vesicle in the cytoplasm. It is believed that a vesicle may carry extracellular fluid to the opposite side of the cell, where it undergoes exocytosis. A droplet of fluid could thus be transported through the cell without disturbing its cytoplasm. Alternatively, the contents of the vesicle may be released to mix with the cytoplasm.

Phagocytosis is a process by which certain living cells called phagocytes ingest or engulf other cells or particles. The phagocyte may be a free-living one-celled organism, such as an amoeba, or one of the body cells, such as a leukocyte (white blood cell). In some forms of animal life, such as amoebas and sponges, phagocytosis is a means of feeding. In higher animals phagocytosis is chiefly a defensive reaction against infection and invasion of the body by foreign substances (antigens).

The particles commonly phagocytosed by leukocytes include bacteria, dead tissue cells, protozoa, various dust particles, pigments, and other minute foreign bodies. In humans, and in vertebrates generally, the most effective phagocytic cells are two kinds of leukocytes: the macrophages (large phagocytic cells) and the neutrophils (a type of granulocyte). The macrophages occur especially in the lungs, liver, spleen, and lymph nodes, where their function is to free the airways, blood, and lymph of bacteria and other particles. Macrophages also are found in all tissues as wandering amoeboid cells, and the monocyte, a precursor of the macrophage, is found in the blood. The smaller phagocytes are chiefly neutrophils that are carried along by the circulating blood until they reach an area of infected tissue, where they pass through the blood vessel

DISCOVERING PHAGOCYTOSIS

Élie Metchnikoff (1845–1916) and Paul Ehrlich received the 1908 Nobel Prize for Physiology or Medicine for their work on immunity. Metchnikoff discovered in animals of amoeba-like cells that engulf foreign bodies such as bacteria—a phenomenon known as phagocytosis and a fundamental part of the immune response. Ehrlich developed a hypothesis to explain immunological phenomena called the side-chain theory, which described how antibodies—the protective proteins produced by the immune system—are formed and how they react with other substances. Delivered to the Royal Society in 1900, this theory was based on an understanding of the way in which a cell was thought to absorb and assimilate nutrients. Although it was ultimately proven to be incorrect in many particulars, it had a profound influence on Ehrlich's later work and the work of his successors.

Metchnikoff contributed to many important discoveries about the immune response. In Messina, Italy (1882–86), while studying the origin of digestive organs in bipinnaria starfish larvae, Metchnikoff observed that certain cells unconnected with digestion surrounded and engulfed carmine dye particles and splinters that he had introduced into the bodies of the larvae. He called these cells phagocytes (from Greek words meaning "devouring cells") and named the process phagocytosis.

Perhaps Metchnikoff's most notable achievement was his recognition that the phagocyte is the first line of defense against acute infection in most animals, including

(Continued on the next page)

(Continued from the previous page)

humans, whose phagocytes are one type of leukocyte, or white blood cell. This work formed the basis of his cellular (phagocytic) theory of immunity (1892), a hypothesis that engendered much opposition, particularly from scientists who claimed that only body fluids and soluble substances in the blood (antibodies)—and not cells—destroyed invading microorganisms (the humoral theory of immunity). Although the humoral theory held sway for the next 50 years, in the 1940s scientists began to reexamine the role cells play in fighting off infections. Eventually Metchnikoff's theory of cellular immunity was vindicated when aspects of both schools of thought became integrated in the modern understanding of immunity.

wall and lodge in that tissue. Both macrophages and neutrophils are drawn toward an area of infection or inflammation by means of substances given off by the bacteria and the infected tissue or by a chemical interaction between the bacteria and the complement system of blood serum proteins. Neutrophils may also engulf particles after colliding with them accidentally.

Before phagocytosis is accomplished, the phagocyte and the particle must adhere to each other, the possibility of which depending largely on the chemical nature of the surface of the particle. If the phagocyte cannot adhere directly, ordinary proteins from the blood can form a surface film on bacteria to which phagocytes adhere, and phago-cytosis follows. Encapsulated bacteria are ingested with more difficulty. Phagocytes, instead of adher-ing to them, succeed only in pushing them away. If, however, the phagocytes succeed in pushing them against a firm surface, such as the lining of a blood vessel, the bacteria may not be able to slip away and, hence, are ingested. This process is known as surface phagocytosis. Other bacteria may not be phagocytosed until their surfaces are coated with special antibodies formed by the body in response to the presence of that particular kind of bacterium. Such antibodies are of great importance in estab-lishing immunity to diseases.

The speed with which a phagocytic cell ingests a particle varies somewhat with the size of the particle. Small particles, such as bacteria or minute grains of charcoal, are ingested almost instantaneously. Larger objects, such as clumps of bacteria or tissue cells, are phagocytosed by a more prolonged response of the leukocyte. The cell flows around the object until it has been completely engulfed. The engulfed object is thus enclosed within a membrane bound vacuole called a phago-some. The phagocyte digests the ingested particle with hydrolytic enzymes, which are contained within membrane-enclosed sacs called lysosomes found within the cell. Phagocytic enzymes are secreted into the vacuole in which digestion takes place.

Small organic components of the particle are used to build larger molecules needed by the cell.

PLANT CELL WALLS

The plant cell wall is a specialized form of extracellular matrix that surrounds every cell of a plant and is responsible for many of the characteristics distinguishing plant cells from animal cells. Although often perceived as an inactive product serving mainly mechanical and structural purposes, the cell wall actually has a multitude of functions upon which plant life depends. Such functions include (1) providing the protoplast, or living cell, with mechanical protection and a chemically buffered environment, (2) providing a porous medium for the circulation and distribution of water, minerals, and other small nutrient molecules, (3) providing rigid building blocks from which stable structures of higher order, such as leaves and stems, can be produced, and (4) providing a storage site of regulatory molecules that sense the presence of pathogenic microbes and control the development of tissues.

MECHANICAL PROPERTIES

All cell walls contain two layers, the middle lamella and the primary cell wall, and many cells produce an additional layer, called the secondary wall. The middle lamella serves as a cementing layer between the

Plant cell

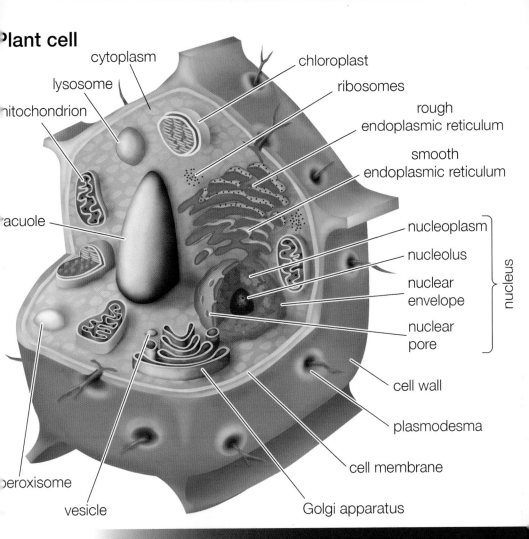

cytoplasm

lysosome

mitochondrion

chloroplast

ribosomes

rough endoplasmic reticulum

smooth endoplasmic reticulum

vacuole

nucleoplasm

nucleolus

nuclear envelope

nuclear pore

nucleus

cell wall

plasmodesma

cell membrane

peroxisome

vesicle

Golgi apparatus

Cutaway drawing of a plant cell, showing the cell wall and internal organelles

primary walls of adjacent cells. The primary wall is the cellulose-containing layer laid down by cells that are dividing and growing. To allow for cell wall expansion during growth, primary walls are thinner and less rigid than those of cells that have stopped growing. A fully grown plant cell may retain its primary cell wall (sometimes thickening it), or it may deposit an additional, rigidifying layer of different composition, which forms the secondary wall. Secondary cell walls are responsible for most of the plant's mechanical support as well as the mechanical properties prized in wood. In contrast to the permanent stiffness and load-bearing capacity of thick secondary walls, the thin primary walls are capable of serving a structural, supportive role only when the vacuoles within the cell are filled with water to the point that they exert a turgor pressure against the cell wall. Turgor-induced stiffening of primary walls is analogous to the stiffening of the sides of a pneumatic tire by air pressure. Flowers and leaves wilt when there is a loss of turgor pressure, which results in turn from the loss of water from the plant cells.

COMPONENTS

Although primary and secondary wall layers differ in detailed chemical composition and structural organization, their basic architecture is the same, consisting of cellulose fibres of great tensile strength embedded in a water-saturated matrix of polysaccharides and structural glycoproteins.

Cellulose

Cellulose consists of several thousand glucose molecules linked end to end. The chemical links between the individual glucose subunits give each cellulose molecule a flat ribbonlike structure that allows adjacent molecules to band laterally together into microfibrils with lengths ranging from two to seven micrometres. Cellulose fibrils are synthesized by enzymes floating in the cell membrane and are arranged in a rosette configuration. Each rosette appears capable of "spinning" a microfibril into the cell wall. During this process, as new glucose subunits are added to the growing end of the fibril, the rosette is pushed around the cell on the surface of the cell membrane, and its cellulose fibril becomes wrapped around the protoplast. Thus, each plant cell can be viewed as making its own cellulose fibril cocoon.

MATRIX POLYSACCHARIDES

The two major classes of cell wall matrix polysaccharides are the hemicelluloses and the pectic polysaccharides, or pectins. Both are synthesized in the Golgi apparatus, brought to the cell surface in small vesicles, and secreted into the cell wall.

Hemicelluloses consist of glucose molecules arranged end to end as in cellulose, with short side chains of xylose and other uncharged sugars attached to one side of the ribbon. The other side of the ribbon binds tightly to the surface of cellulose fibrils, thereby coating the microfibrils with hemicellulose and preventing them from adhering together in an uncontrolled manner. Hemicellulose molecules have been shown to regulate the rate at which primary cell walls expand during growth.

The heterogeneous, branched, and highly hydrated pectic polysaccharides differ from hemicelluloses in important respects. Most notably, they are negatively charged because of galacturonic acid residues, which, together with rhamnose sugar molecules, form the linear backbone of all pectic polysaccharides. The backbone contains stretches of pure galacturonic acid residues interrupted by segments in which galacturonic acid and rhamnose residues alternate. Attached to these latter segments are complex, branched sugar side chains. Because of their negative charge, pectic polysaccharides bind tightly to positively charged ions, or cations. In cell walls, calcium ions cross-link the stretches of pure galacturonic acid residues tightly, while leaving the rhamnose-containing segments in a more open, porous configuration. This cross-linking creates the semirigid gel properties characteristic of the cell wall matrix—a process exploited in the preparation of jellied preserves.

CELL WALL PROTEINS

Although plant cell walls contain only small amounts of protein, they serve a number of important functions. The most prominent group are the hydroxyproline-rich glycoproteins, shaped like rods with connector sites, of which extensin is a prominent example. Extensin contains 45 percent hydroxyproline and 14 percent serine residues distributed along its length. Every hydroxyproline residue carries a short side chain of arabinose sugars, and most serine residues carry a galactose sugar. This gives rise to long molecules, resembling bottle brushes, that are secreted into the cell wall toward the end of primary-wall formation and become covalently cross-linked into a mesh at the time that cell growth stops. Plant cells may control their ultimate size by regulating the time at which this cross-linking of extensin molecules occurs.

In addition to the structural proteins, cell walls contain a variety of enzymes. Most notable are those that cross-link extensin, lignin, cutin, and suberin molecules into networks. Other enzymes help protect plants against fungal pathogens by breaking fragments off of the cell walls of the fungi. The fragments in turn induce defense responses in underlying cells. The softening of ripe fruit and dropping of leaves in the autumn are brought about by cell wall-degrading enzymes.

CELL WALL PLASTICS

Cell wall plastics such as lignin, cutin, and suberin all contain a variety of organic compounds cross-linked into tight three-dimensional networks that strengthen cell walls and make them more resistant to fungal and bacterial attack. Lignin is the general name for a diverse group of polymers of aromatic alcohols. Deposited mostly in secondary cell walls and providing the rigidity of terrestrial vascular plants, it accounts for up to 30 percent of a plant's dry weight. The diversity of cross-links between the polymers—and the resulting tightness—makes lignin a formidable barrier to the penetration of most microbes. Cutin and suberin are complex biopolyesters composed of fatty acids and aromatic compounds. Cutin is the major component of the cuticle, the waxy, water-repelling surface layer of cell walls exposed to the environment aboveground. By reducing the wetability of leaves and stems—and thereby affecting the ability of fungal spores to germinate—it plays an important part in the defense strategy of plants. Suberin serves with waxes as a surface barrier of underground parts. Its synthesis is also stimulated in cells close to wounds, thereby sealing off the wound surfaces and protecting underlying cells from dehydration.

CELLULAR ORGANELLES

A cell with its many different DNA, RNA, and protein molecules is quite different from a test tube containing the same components. When a cell is dissolved in a test tube, thousands of different types of molecules randomly mix together. In the living cell, however, these components are kept in specific places, reflecting the high degree of organization essential for the growth and division of the cell. Maintaining this internal organization requires a continuous input of energy, because spontaneous chemical reactions always create disorganization. Thus, much of the energy released by ATP hydrolysis fuels processes that organize macromolecules inside the cell.

When a eukaryotic cell is examined at high magnification in an electron microscope, it becomes apparent that specific membrane-bound organelles divide the interior into a variety of subcompartments. Although not detectable in the electron microscope, it is clear from biochemical assays that each organelle contains a different set of macromolecules. This biochemical segregation reflects the functional specialization of each compartment. Thus, the mitochondria, which produce most of the cell's ATP, contain all of the enzymes needed to carry out the tricarboxylic acid cycle and oxidative phosphorylation. Similarly, the degradative enzymes needed for the intracellular digestion of unwanted macromolecules are confined to the lysosomes.

It is clear from this functional segregation that the many different proteins specified by the genes in the cell nucleus must be transported to the compartment where they will be used. Not surprisingly, the cell contains an extensive membrane-bound system devoted to maintaining just this intracellular order. The system serves as a post office, guaranteeing the proper routing of newly synthesized macromolecules to their proper destinations.

All proteins are synthesized on ribosomes located in the cytosol. As soon as the first portion of the amino acid sequence of a protein emerges from the ribosome, it is inspected for the presence of a short "endoplasmic reticulum (ER) signal sequence." Those ribosomes making proteins with such a sequence are transported to the surface of the ER membrane, where they complete their synthesis.

The proteins made on these ribosomes are immediately transferred through the ER membrane to the inside of the ER compartment. Proteins lacking the ER signal sequence remain in the cytosol and are released from the ribosomes when their synthesis is completed. This chemical decision process places some newly completed protein chains in the cytosol and others within an extensive membrane bounded compartment in the cytoplasm, representing the first step in intracellular protein sorting.

The newly made proteins in both cell compartments are then sorted further according to additional signal sequences that they contain. Some of the proteins in the cytosol remain there, while others go to the surface of mitochondria or (in plant cells) chloroplasts, where they are transferred through the membranes into the organelles. Subsignals on each of these proteins then designate exactly where in the organelle the protein belongs. The proteins initially sorted into the ER have an even wider range of destinations. Some of them remain in the ER, where they function as part of the organelle. Most enter transport vesicles and pass to the Golgi apparatus, separate membrane-bounded organelles that contain at least three subcompartments. Some of the proteins are retained in the subcompartments of the Golgi, where they are utilized for functions peculiar to that organelle. Most eventually enter vesicles that leave the Golgi for other cellular destinations such as the cell membrane, lysosomes, or special secretory vesicles.

INTERNAL MEMBRANES

The presence of internal membranes distinguishes eukaryotic cells (cells with a nucleus) from prokaryotic cells (those without a nucleus). Prokaryotic cells are small (one to five micrometres in length) and contain only a single cell membrane. Metabolic functions are often confined to different patches of the membrane rather than to areas in the body of the cell. Typical eukaryotic cells, by contrast, are much larger, the cell membrane constituting only 10 percent or less of the total cellular membrane. Metabolic functions in these cells are carried out in the organelles, compartments sequestered from the cell body, or cytoplasm, by internal membranes.

The principal organelles are the nucleus, the mitochondrion, and (in plants) the chloroplast. Of the remaining organelles, the lysosomes, peroxisomes, and (in plants) glyoxysomes enclose extremely reactive by-products and enzymes. Internal membranes form the mazelike endoplasmic reticulum, where cell membrane proteins and lipids are synthesized, and they also form the stacks of flattened sacs called the Golgi apparatus, which is associated with the transport and modification of lipids, proteins, and carbo-

hydrates. Finally, internal cell membranes can form storage and transport vesicles and the vacuoles of plant cells. Each membrane structure has its own distinct composition of proteins and lipids enabling it to carry out unique functions.

Similar to the cell membrane, membranes of some organelles contain transport proteins, or permeases, that allow chemical communication between organelles. Permeases in the lysosomal membrane, for example, allow amino acids generated inside the lysosome to cross into the cytoplasm, where they can be used for the synthesis of new proteins. Communication between organelles is also achieved by the membrane budding processes of endocytosis and exocytosis, which are essentially the same as in the cell membrane. Conversely, the biosynthetic and degradative processes taking place in different organelles may require conditions greatly different from those of other organelles or of the cytosol (the fluid part of the cell surrounding the organelles). Internal membranes maintain these different conditions by isolating them from one another. For example, the internal space of lysosomes is much more acidic than that of the cytosol—pH 5 as opposed to pH 7—and is maintained by specific protonpumping transport proteins in the lysosome membrane.

Another function of organelles is to prevent competing enzymatic reactions from interfering with one another. For instance, essential proteins are

synthesized on the rough endoplasmic reticulum and in the cytosol, while unwanted proteins are broken down in the lysosomes and also, to some extent, in the cytosol. Similarly, fatty acids are made in the cytosol and then either broken down in the mitochondria for the synthesis of ATP or degraded in the peroxisomes with concomitant generation of heat. These processes must be kept isolated. Organelle membranes also prevent potentially lethal by-products or enzymes from attacking sensitive molecules in other regions of the cell by sequestering such degradative activities in their respective membrane-bounded compartments.

The internal membranes of eukaryotic cells differ both structurally and chemically from the outer cell membrane. Like the outer membrane, they are constructed of a phospholipid bilayer into which are embedded, or bound, specific membrane proteins. The three major lipids forming the outer membrane—phospholipids, cholesterol, and glycolipids—are also found in the internal membranes, but in different concentrations. Phospholipid is the primary lipid forming all cellular membranes. Cholesterol, which contributes to the fluidity and stability of all membranes, is found in internal membranes at about 25 percent of the concentration in the outer membrane. Glycolipids are found only as trace components of internal membranes, whereas they constitute approximately 5 percent of the outer membrane lipid.

NUCLEUS

The nucleus is the information centre of the cell and is surrounded by a nuclear membrane in all eukaryotic organisms. It is separated from the cytoplasm by the nuclear envelope, and it houses the double-stranded, spiral-shaped DNA molecules, which contain the genetic information necessary for the cell to retain its unique character as it grows and divides.

The presence of a nucleus distinguishes the eukaryotic cells of multicellular organisms from the prokaryotic, one-celled organisms such as bacteria. In contrast to the higher organisms, prokaryotes do not have nuclei, so their DNA is maintained in the same compartment as their other cellular components.

The primary function of the nucleus is the expression of selected subsets of the genetic information encoded in the DNA double helix. Each subset of a DNA chain, called a gene, codes for the construction of a specific protein out of a chain of amino acids. Information in DNA is not decoded directly into proteins, however. First it is transcribed, or copied, into a range of messenger ribonucleic acid (mRNA) molecules, each of which encodes the information for one protein (or more than one protein in bacteria). The mRNA molecules are then transported through the nuclear envelope into the cytoplasm, where they are translated, serving as templates for the synthesis of specific proteins.

The nucleus must not only synthesize the mRNA for many thousands of proteins, but it must also regulate the amounts synthesized and supplied to the cytoplasm. Furthermore, the amounts of each type of mRNA supplied to the cytoplasm must be regulated differently in each type of cell. In addition to mRNA, the nucleus synthesizes and exports other classes of RNA involved in the mechanisms of protein synthesis.

DNA PACKAGING

The nucleus of the average human cell is only 6 micrometres (6×10^{-6} metre) in diameter, yet it contains about 1.8 metres (5.9 feet) of DNA. This is distributed among 46 chromosomes, each consisting of a single DNA molecule about 40 mm (1.5 inches) long. The extraordinary packaging problem this poses can be envisaged by a scale model enlarged a million times. On this scale a DNA molecule would be a thin string 2 mm thick, and the average chromosome would contain 40 km (25 miles) of DNA. With a diameter of only 6 metres, the nucleus would contain 1,800 km (1,118 miles) of DNA.

These contents must be organized in such a way that they can be copied into RNA accurately and selectively. DNA is not simply crammed or wound into the nucleus like a ball of string. Rather, it is

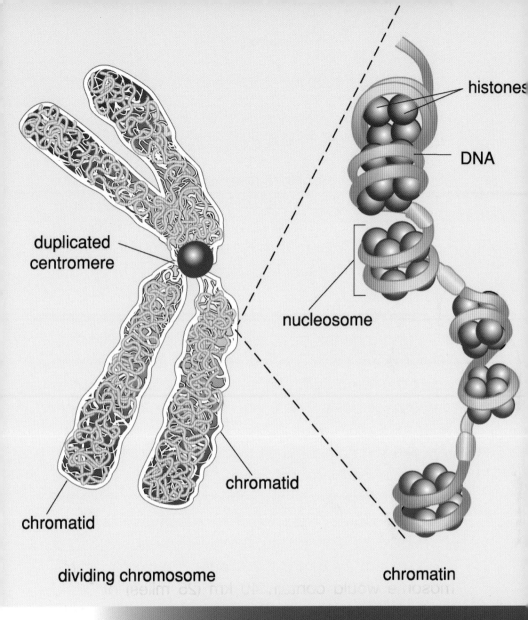

histones

DNA

duplicated centromere

nucleosome

chromatid

chromatid

dividing chromosome

chromatin

During the first stages of cell division, the recognizable double-stranded chromosome is formed by two tightly coiled DNA strands (chromatids) joined at a point called the centromere. During the middle stage of cell division, the centromere duplicates, and the chromatid pair separates. Following cell division, the separated chromatids uncoil; the loosely coiled DNA, wrapped around its associated proteins (histones) to form beaded structures called nucleosomes, is termed chromatin.

organized, by molecular interaction with specific nuclear proteins, into a precisely packaged structure. This combination of DNA with proteins creates a dense, compact fibre called chromatin. An extreme example of the ordered folding and compaction that chromatin can undergo is seen during cell division, when the chromatin of each chromosome condenses and is divided between two daughter cells.

The compaction of DNA is achieved by winding it around a series of small proteins called histones. Histones are composed of positively charged amino acids that bind tightly to and neutralize the negative charges of DNA. There are five classes of histone. Four of them, called H2A, H2B, H3, and H4, contribute two molecules each to form an octamer, an eight-part core around which two turns of DNA are wrapped. The resulting beadlike structure is called the nucleosome. The DNA enters and leaves a series of nucleosomes, linking them like beads along a string in lengths that vary between species of organism or even between different types of cell within a species. A string of nucleosomes is then coiled into a solenoid configuration by the fifth histone, called H1. One molecule of H1 binds to the site at which DNA enters and leaves each nucleosome, and a chain of H1 molecules coils the string of nucleosomes into the solenoid structure of the chromatin fibre.

Nucleosomes not only neutralize the charges of DNA, but they have other consequences. First, they are an efficient means of packaging. DNA becomes compacted by a factor of six when wound into nucleosomes and by a factor of about 40 when the nucleosomes are coiled into a solenoid chromatin fibre. The winding into nucleosomes also allows some inactive DNA to be folded away in inaccessible conformations, a process that contributes to the selectivity of gene expression.

Several studies indicate that chromatin is organized into a series of large radial loops anchored to specific scaffold proteins. Each loop consists of a chain of nucleosomes and may be related to units of genetic organization. This radial arrangement of chromatin loops compacts DNA about a thousandfold. Further compaction is achieved by a coiling of the entire looped chromatin fibre into a dense structure called a chromatid, two of which form the chromosome. During cell division, this coiling produces a 10,000-fold compaction of DNA.

NUCLEAR ENVELOPE

The nuclear envelope is a double membrane composed of an outer and an inner phospholipid bilayer. The thin space between the two layers connects with the lumen of the rough endoplasmic reticulum (RER), and the outer layer is an extension of the outer face of the RER.

The inner surface of the nuclear envelope has a protein lining called the nuclear lamina, which binds to chromatin and other contents of the nucleus. The entire envelope is perforated by numerous nuclear pores. These transport routes are fully permeable to small molecules up to the size of the smallest proteins, but they form a selective barrier against movement of larger molecules. Each pore is surrounded by an elaborate protein structure called the nuclear pore complex, which selects molecules for entrance into the nucleus. Entering the nucleus through the pores are the nucleotide building blocks of DNA and RNA, as well as adenosine triphosphate, which provides the energy for synthesizing genetic material. Histones and other large proteins must also pass through the pores. These molecules have special amino acid sequences on their surface that signal admittance by the nuclear pore complexes. The complexes also regulate the export from the nucleus of RNA and subunits of ribosomes. DNA in prokaryotes is also organized in loops and is bound to small proteins resembling histones, but these structures are not enclosed by a nuclear membrane.

GENETIC ORGANIZATION

The configuration and organization of the DNA molecule within the cell nucleus influences the mechanisms utilized by eukaryotic organisms for DNA replication. The processes of DNA replication and modification in turn influence the structure and function of cells. In addition, because DNA codes genetic information for the transmission of inherited traits, the mechanisms regulating its replication and modification play a fundamental role in determining the genetic characteristics of an organism's offspring.

THE STRUCTURE OF DNA

Several features are common to the genetic structure of most organisms. First is the double-stranded DNA. Each strand of this molecule is a series of nucleotides, and each nucleotide is composed of a sugar-phosphate compound attached to one of four nitrogen-containing bases. The sugar-phosphate compounds link together to form the backbone of the strand. Each base strung along the backbone is chemically attracted to a corresponding base on the parallel strand of the DNA molecule. This base pairing joins the two strands of the molecule much as rungs join the two sides of a ladder, and the chemical bonding of the base pairs twists the doubled strands into a spiral, or helical, shape.

The four nucleotide bases are adenine, cytosine, guanine, and thymine. DNA is composed of millions of these bases strung in an apparently limitless variety of sequences. It is in the sequence of bases that the genetic information is contained, each sequence determining the sequence of amino acids to be connected into proteins. A nucleotide sequence sufficient to encode one protein is called a gene. Genes are interspersed along the DNA molecule with other sequences that do not encode proteins. Some of these so-called untranslated regions regulate the activity of the adjacent genes, for example, by marking the points at which enzymes begin and cease transcribing DNA into RNA.

REARRANGEMENT AND MODIFICATION OF DNA

Rearrangements and modifications of the nucleotide sequences in DNA are exceptions to the rules of genetic expression and sometimes cause significant changes in the structure and function of cells. Different cells of the body owe their specialized structures and functions to different genes. This does not mean that the set of genetic information varies among the cells of the body. Indeed, for each cell the entire DNA content of the chromosomes is usually duplicated exactly from generation to generation, and, in general, the genetic content and arrangement is strikingly similar among different cell types of the same organism. As a result, the differentiation of cells can occur without the loss or irreversible inactivation of unnecessary genes, an observation that is reinforced by the presence of specific genes in a range of adult tissues. For example, normal copies of the genes encoding hemoglobin are present in the same numbers in red blood cells, which make hemoglobin, as in a range of other types of cells, which do not.

Despite the general uniformity of genetic content in all the cells of an organism, studies have shown a few clear examples in some organisms of programmed, reversible change in the DNA of developing tissues. One of the most dramatic rearrangements of DNA occurs in the immune systems of mammals. The body's defense against invasion by foreign organisms involves the synthesis of a vast range of antibodies by lymphocytes (a type of white blood cell). Antibodies are proteins that bind to specific invading molecules or organisms and either inactivate them or signal their destruction. The binding sites on each antibody molecule are formed by one light and one heavy amino acid chain, which are encoded by different segments of the DNA in the lymphocyte nucleus. These DNA segments undergo considerable rearrangements, resulting in the synthesis of a great variety of antibodies. Some invasive organisms, such as trypanosome parasites, which cause sleeping sickness, go to great lengths to rearrange their own DNA to evade the versatility of their hosts' antibody production. The parasites are covered by a thick coat of glycoprotein (a protein with sugars attached). Given time, host organisms can overcome infection by producing antibodies to the parasites' glycoprotein coat, but this reaction is anticipated and evaded by the selective rearrangement of the trypanosomes' DNA encoding the glycoprotein, thus constantly changing the surface presented to the hosts' immune system.

Careful comparisons of gene structure have also revealed epigenetic modifications, heritable changes that occur on the sugar-phosphate side of bases in the DNA and thus do not cause rearrangements in the DNA sequence itself. An example of an epigenetic modification involves the addition of a methyl group to cytosine bases. This appears to cause the inactivation of genes that do not need to be expressed in a particular type of cell. An important feature of the methylation of cytosine lies in its ability to be copied, so that methyl groups in a dividing cell's DNA will result in methyl groups in the same positions in the DNA of both daughter cells.

GENETIC EXPRESSION THROUGH RNA

The transcription of the genetic code from DNA to RNA, and the translation of that code from RNA into protein, exerts the greatest influence on the modulation of genetic information. The process of genetic expression takes place over several stages, and at each stage is the potential for further differentiation of cell types.

As explained previously, genetic information is encoded in the sequences of the four nucleotide bases making up a DNA molecule. One of the two DNA strands is transcribed exactly into mRNA, with the exception that the thymine base of DNA is replaced by uracil. RNA also contains a slightly different sugar component (ribose) from that of DNA (deoxyribose) in its connecting sugar-phosphate chain. Unlike DNA, which is stable throughout the cell's life and of which individual strands are even passed on to many cell generations, RNA is unstable. It is continuously broken down and replaced, enabling the cell to change its patterns of protein synthesis.

Apart from mRNA, which encodes proteins, other classes of RNA are made by the nucleus. These include ribosomal RNA (rRNA), which forms part of the ribosomes and is exported to the cytoplasm to help translate the information in mRNA into proteins. Ribosomal RNA is synthesized in a specialized region of the nucleus called the nucleolus, which appears as a dense area within the nucleus and contains the genes that encode rRNA. This is also the site of assembly of ribosome subunits from rRNA and ribosomal proteins. Ribosomal proteins are synthesized in the cytoplasm and transported to the nucleus for subassembly in the nucleolus. The subunits are then returned to the cytoplasm for final assembly. Another class of RNA synthesized in the nucleus is transfer RNA (tRNA), which serves as an adaptor, matching individual amino acids to the nucleotide triplets of mRNA during protein synthesis.

RNA SYNTHESIS

The synthesis of RNA is performed by enzymes called RNA polymerases. In higher organisms there are three main RNA polymerases, designated I, II, and III (or sometimes A, B, and C). Each is a complex protein consisting of many subunits. RNA polymerase I synthesizes three of the four types of rRNA (called 18S, 28S, and 5.8S RNA). Therefore it is active in the nucleolus, where the genes encoding these rRNA molecules reside. RNA polymerase II synthesizes mRNA, though its initial products are not mature RNA but larger precursors, called heterogeneous nuclear RNA, which are completed later. The products of RNA polymerase III include tRNA and the fourth RNA component of the ribosome, called 5S RNA.

All three polymerases start RNA synthesis at specific sites on DNA and proceed along the molecule, linking selected nucleotides sequentially until they come to the end ofthe gene and terminate the growing chain of RNA. Energy for RNA synthesis comes from high-energy phosphate linkages contained in the nucleotide precursors of RNA. Each unit of the final RNA product is essentially a sugar, a base, and one phosphate, but the building material consists of a sugar, a base, and three phosphates. During synthesis two phosphates are cleaved and discarded for each nucleotide that is incorporated into RNA.The energy released from the phosphate bonds is used to link the nucleotides. The crucial feature of RNA synthesis is that the sequence of nucleotides joined into a growing RNA chain is specified by the sequence of nucleotides in the DNA template: Each adenine in DNA specifies uracil in RNA, each cytosine specifies guanine, each guanine specifies cytosine, and each thymine in DNA specifies adenine. In this way the information encoded in each gene is transcribed into RNA for translation by the protein-synthesizing machinery of the cytoplasm.

In addition to specifying the sequence of amino acids to be polymerized into proteins, the nucleotide sequence of DNA contains supplementary information. For example, short sequences of nucleotides determine the initiation site for each RNA polymerase, specifying where and when RNA synthesis should occur. In the case of RNA polymerases I and II, the sequences specifying initiation sites lie just ahead of the genes. In contrast, the equivalent information for RNA polymerase III lies within the gene—that is, within the region of DNA to be copied into RNA. The initiation site on a segment of DNA is called a promoter. The promoters of different genes have some nucleotide sequences in common, but they differ in others. The differences in sequence are recognized by specific proteins called transcription factors, which are necessary for the expression of particular types of genes. The specificity of transcription factors contributes to differences in the gene expression of different types of cells.

PROCESSING OF mRNA

During and after synthesis, mRNA precursors undergo a complex series of changes before the mature molecules are released from the nucleus. First, a modified nucleotide is added to the start of the RNA molecule by a reaction called capping. This cap later binds to a ribosome in the cytoplasm. The synthesis of mRNA is not terminated simply by the RNA polymerase's detachment from DNA, but by chemical cleavage of the RNA chain. Many (but not all) types of mRNA have a simple polymer of adenosine residues added to their cleaved ends.

In addition to these modifications of the termini, startling discoveries in 1977 revealed that portions of newly synthesized RNA molecules are cut out and discarded. In many genes, the regions coding for

proteins are interrupted by intervening sequences of nucleotides called introns. These introns must be excised from the RNA copy before it can be released from the nucleus as a functional mRNA. The number and size of introns within a gene vary greatly, from no introns at all to more than 50. The sum of the lengths of these intervening sequences is sometimes longer than the sum of the regions coding for proteins.

The removal of introns, called RNA splicing, appears to be mediated by small nuclear ribonucleoprotein particles (snRNPs). These particles have RNA sequences that are complementary to the junctions between introns and adjacent coding regions. By binding to the junction ends, an snRNP twists the intron into a loop. It then excises the loop and splices the coding regions.

REGULATION OF GENETIC EXPRESSION AND RNA SYNTHESIS

Although all the cell nuclei of an organism generally carry the same genes, there are conspicuous differences between the specialized cell types of the body. The source of these differences lies not so much in the occasional modification of DNA, but in the selective expression of DNA through RNA. In particular, it can be traced to processes regulating the amounts and activities of mRNA both during and after its synthesis in the nucleus.

The first level of regulation is mediated by variations in chromatin structure. In order to be transcribed, a gene must be assembled into a structurally distinct form of active chromatin. A second level of regulation is achieved by varying the frequency with which a gene in the active conformation is transcribed into RNA by an RNA polymerase. There is evidence for regulation of RNA synthesis at both these levels—for example, in response to hormone induction. At both levels, protein factors are believed to perform the regulation—for example, by binding to special promoter DNA regions flanking the transcribed gene.

After synthesis, RNA molecules undergo selective processing, which results in the export of only a subpopulation of RNA molecules to the cytoplasm. Furthermore, the stability in the cytoplasm of a particular type of mRNA can be regulated. For example, the hormone prolactin increases synthesis of milk proteins in tissue by causing a twofold rise in the rate of mRNA synthesis. But prolactin also causes a 17-fold rise in mRNA lifetime, so that in this case the main cause of increased protein synthesis is the prolonged availability of mRNA. Conversely, there is evidence for selective destabilization of some mRNA—such as histone mRNA, which is rapidly broken down when DNA replication is interrupted. Finally, there are many examples of selective regulation of the translation of mRNA into protein.

MITOCHONDRIA AND CHLOROPLASTS

Mitochondria and chloroplasts are the powerhouses of the cell. Mitochondria appear in both plant and animal cells as elongated cylindrical bodies, roughly one micrometer in length and closely packed in regions actively using metabolic energy. Mitochondria oxidize the products of cytoplasmic metabolism to generate ATP, the energy currency of the cell. Chloroplasts are the photosynthetic organelles in plants and some algae. They trap light energy and convert it partly into ATP but mainly into certain chemically reduced molecules that, together with ATP, are used in the first steps of carbohydrate production. Mitochondria and chloroplasts share a certain structural resemblance, and both have a somewhat independent existence within the cell, synthesizing some proteins from instructions supplied by their own DNA.

STRUCTURE

Both organelles are bounded by an external membrane that serves as a barrier by blocking the passage of cytoplasmic proteins into the organelle. An inner membrane provides an additional barrier that is impermeable even to small ions such as protons. The membranes of both organelles have a lipid bilayer construction. Located between the inner and outer membranes is the inter membrane space.

In mitochondria the inner membrane is elaborately folded into structures called cristae that dramatically increase the surface area of the membrane. In contrast, the inner membrane of chloroplasts is relatively smooth. However, within this membrane is yet another series of folded membranes that form a set of flattened, disklike sacs called thylakoids. The space enclosed by the inner membrane is called the matrix in mitochondria and the stroma in chloroplasts. Both spaces are filled with a fluid containing a rich mixture of metabolic products, enzymes, and ions. Enclosed by the thylakoid membrane of the chloroplast is the thylakoid space. The extraordinary chemical capabilities of the two organelles lie in the cristae and the thylakoids. Both membranes are studded with enzymatic proteins either traversing the bilayer or dissolved within the bilayer. These proteins contribute to the production of energy by transporting material across the membranes and by serving as electron carriers in important oxidation-reduction reactions.

METABOLIC FUNCTIONS

Crucial to the function of mitochondria and chloroplasts is the chemistry of the oxidation-reduction, or redox, reaction. This controlled burning of material comprises the transfer of electrons from one compound, called the donor, to another, called the

acceptor. All compounds taking part in redox reactions are ranked in a descending scale according to their ability to act as electron donors. Those higher in the scale donate electrons to their fellows lower down, which have a lesser tendency to donate, but a correspondingly greater tendency to accept, electrons. Each acceptor in turn donates electrons to the next compound down the scale, forming a donor-acceptor chain extending from the greatest donating ability to the least.

At the top of the scale is hydrogen, the most abundant element in the universe. The nucleus of a hydrogen atom is composed of one positively charged proton. Around the nucleus revolves one negatively charged electron. In the atmosphere two hydrogen atoms join to form a hydrogen molecule (H_2). In solution the two atoms pull apart, dissociating into their constituent protons and electrons.

In the redox reaction the electrons are passed from one reactant to another. The donation of electrons is called oxidation, and the acceptance is called reduction—hence the descriptive term oxidation-reduction, indicating that one action never takes place without the other.

A hydrogen atom has a great tendency to transfer an electron to an acceptor. An oxygen atom, in contrast, has a great tendency to accept an electron. The burning of hydrogen by oxygen is, chemically, the transfer of an electron from each of two hydrogen atoms to oxygen, so that hydrogen is oxidized and oxygen reduced. The reaction is extremely exergonic—it liberates much free energy as heat. This is the reaction that takes place within mitochondria, but it is so controlled that the heat is liberated not at once but in a series of steps. The free energy, harnessed by the organelle, is coupled to the synthesis of ATP from adenosine diphosphate (ADP) and inorganic phosphate (P_i).

An analogy can be drawn between this controlled reaction and the flow of river water down a lock system. Without the locks, water flow would be rapid and uncontrolled, and no ship could safely ply the river. The locks force water to flow in small controlled steps conducive to safe navigation. But there is more to a lock system than this. The flow of water down the locks can also be harnessed to raise a ship from a lower to a higher level, with the water rather than the ship expending the energy. In mitochondria, the burning of hydrogen is broken into a series of small indirect steps following the flow of electrons along a chain of donor-acceptors. Energy is funneled into the chemical bonding of ADP and P_i, raising the free energy of these two compounds to the high level of ATP.

MITOCHONDRIAL ELECTRON TRANSPORT

Through a series of metabolic reactions carried out in the matrix, the mitochondrion converts products of the cell's initial metabolism of fats, amino acids, and sugars into the compound acetyl coenzyme A. The acetate portion of this compound is then oxidized in a chain reaction called the tricarboxylic acid cycle. At the end of this cycle, the carbon atoms yield carbon dioxide and the hydrogen atoms are transferred to the cell's most important hydrogen acceptors, the coenzymes nicotinamide adenine dinucleotide (NAD^+) and flavin adenine dinucleotide (FAD), yielding NADH and $FADH_2$. The subsequent oxidation of these hydrogen acceptors eventually leads to the production of ATP.

NADH and $FADH_2$ are compounds of high electron-donating capacity. Were they to transfer their electrons directly to oxygen, the resulting combustion would release a lethal burst of heat energy. Instead, the energy is released in a series of electron donor-acceptor reactions carried out within the cristae of the mitochondrion by a number of proteins and coenzymes that make up the electron transport, or respiratory, chain.

The proteins of this chain are embedded in the cristae membrane, actually traversing the lipid bilayer and protruding from the inner and outer surfaces. The coenzymes are dissolved in the lipid and diffuse through the membrane or across its surface. The proteins are arranged in three large complexes, each composed of a number of polypeptide chains. Each complex is, to continue the hydraulic analogy, a lock in the waterfall of the electron flow and the site at which energy from the overall redox reaction is tapped. The first complex, NADH dehydrogenase, accepts a pair of electrons from the primary electron donor NADH and is reduced in the process. It in turn donates these electrons to the coenzyme ubiquinone, a lipid-soluble molecule composed of a substituted benzene ring attached to a hydrocarbon tail. Ubiquinone, diffusing through the lipid of the cristae membrane, reaches the second large

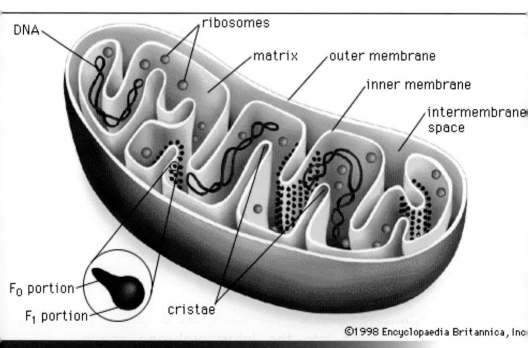

DNA

ribosomes

matrix · outer membrane

inner membrane

intermembrane space

F_0 portion

F_1 portion

cristae

©1998 Encyclopaedia Britannica, Inc

The internal membrane of a mitochondrion is elaborately folded into structures known as cristae. Cristae increase the surface area of the inner membrane, which houses the components of the electron-transport chain. Proteins known as F_1F_0 ATPases that produce the majority of ATP used by cells are found throughout the cristae.

complex of the electron-transport chain, the b-c2 complex, which accepts the electrons, oxidizing ubiquinone and being itself reduced. (This complex can also accept electrons from the second primary electron donor, $FADH_2$, a molecule below NADH in the electron-donating scale.) The b-c2 complex transfers the pair of electrons to cytochrome c, a small protein situated on the outer surface of the cristae membrane. From cytochrome c, electrons pass (four at a time) to the third large complex, cytochrome oxidase, which, in the final step of the chain, transfers the four electrons to two oxygen atoms and two protons, generating two water molecules.

This transfer of electrons, from member to member of the electron-transport chain, provides energy for the synthesis of ATP through an indirect route. At the beginning of the electron-transport chain, NADH and $FADH_2$ split hydrogen atoms into protons and electrons, transferring the electrons to the next protein complex and releasing the protons into the mitochondrial matrix. When each protein complex in turn transfers the electrons down the chain, it uses the energy released in this process to pump protons across the inner membrane into the intermembrane space. This transport of positively charged protons into the intermembrane space, opposite the negatively charged electrons in the matrix, creates an electrical potential that tends to draw the protons back across the membrane. A high concentration of protons outside the membrane also creates the conditions for their diffusion back into the matrix. However, as already explained, the inner membrane is extremely impermeable to protons. For the protons to flow back down the electrochemical gradient, they must traverse the membrane through transport molecules similar to the protein complexes of the electron-transfer chain. These molecules are the so-called F_1F_0ATPase, a complex protein that, transporting protons back into the matrix, uses the energy released to synthesize ATP. The protons then join the electrons and oxygen atoms to form water.

This complex chain of events, the basis of the cell's ability to derive ATP from metabolic oxidation, was conceived in its entirety by British biochemist Peter Mitchell in 1961. The years following the announcement of his chemiosmotic theory saw its ample substantiation and revealed its profound implications for cell biology.

THE CHEMIOSMOTIC THEORY

The four postulates of the chemiosmotic theory, including examples of their experimental substantiation, are as follows:

1. The inner mitochondrial membrane is impermeable to protons, hydroxide ions, and other cations and anions. This postulate was val-

idated when it was shown that substances allowing protons to flow readily across mitochondrial membranes uncouple oxidative electron transport from ATP production.

2. Transfer of electrons down the electron transport chain brings about pumping of protons across the inner membrane, from matrix to intermembrane space. This was demonstrated in laboratory experiments that reconstituted the components of the electron-transport chain in artificial membrane vesicles. The stimulation of electron transport caused a measurable buildup of protons within the vesicle.

3. The flow of protons down a built-up electrochemical gradient occurs through a proton-dependent ATPase, so that ATP is synthesized from ADP and P_i whenever protons move through the enzyme. This hypothesis was confirmed by the discovery of what came to be known as the F_1F_0ATPase. Shaped like a knob attached to the membrane by a narrow stalk, F_1F_0ATPase covers the inner surface of the cristae. Its stalk (the F_0 portion) penetrates the lipid bilayer of the inner membrane and is capable of catalyzing the transport of protons. The knob (the F_1 portion) is capable of synthesizing as well as splitting, or hydrolyzing, ATP. F_1F_0ATPase is therefore reversible,

either using the energy of proton diffusion to combine ADP and P_i or using the energy of ATP hydrolysis to pump protons out of the matrix.

4. The inner membrane of the mitochondrion possesses a complement of proteins that brings about the transport of essential metabolites. Numerous carrier systems have been demonstrated to transport into the mitochondrion the products of metabolism that are transformed into substrates for the electron-transport chain. Best known is the ATP-ADP exchange carrier of the inner membrane. Neither ATP nor ADP, being large charged molecules, can cross the membrane unaided, but ADP must enter and ATP must leave the mitochondrial matrix for ATP synthesis to continue. A single protein conducts the counter-transport of ATP against ADP, the energy released by the flow of ATP down its concentration gradient being coupled to the pumping of ADP up its gradient and into the mitochondrion.

CHLOROPLASTS: TRAPPING LIGHT AND FIXATION OF CARBON DIOXIDE

Light travels as packets of energy known as photons and is absorbed in this form by light-absorbing chlorophyll molecules embedded in the thylakoid membrane of the chloroplast. The chlorophyll molecules are grouped into antenna complexes, clusters of several hundred molecules that are anchored onto the thylakoid membrane by special proteins. Within each antenna complex is a specialized set of proteins and chlorophyll molecules that form a reaction centre. Photons absorbed by the other chlorophylls of the antenna are funneled into the reaction centre. The energy of the photon is absorbed by an electron of the reaction centre molecule in sufficient quantity to enable its acceptance by a nearby coenzyme, which cannot accept electrons at low energy levels. This coenzyme has a high electrondonor capability. It initiates the transfer of the electron down an electron-transport chain similar to that of the mitochondrion.

Meanwhile, the loss of the negatively charged electron leaves a positively charged "hole" in the reaction centre chlorophyll molecule. This hole is filled by the enzymatic splitting of water into molecular oxygen, protons, and electrons and the transfer of an electron to the chlorophyll. The oxygen is released by the chloroplast, making its way out of the plant and into the atmosphere. The protons, in a process similar to that in the mitochondrion, are pumped through the thylakoid membrane and into the thylakoid space. Their facilitated diffusion back into the stroma through proteins embedded in the

The reaction of photosynthesis

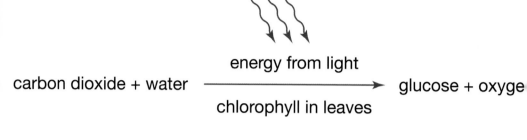

carbon dioxide + water $\xrightarrow[\text{chlorophyll in leaves}]{\text{energy from light}}$ glucose + oxyge

$$6CO_2 + 6H_2O \longrightarrow C_6H_{12}O_6 + 6O_2$$

In photosynthesis, plants consume carbon dioxide and water and produce glucose and oxygen. Energy for this process is provided by light, which is absorbed by pigments, primarily chlorophyll. Chlorophyll is the pigment that gives plants their green colour.

membrane powers the synthesis of ATP. This part of the photosynthetic process is called photosystem II.

At the end of the electron-transport chain in the thylakoid membrane is another reaction centre molecule. The electron is again energized by photons and then transported down another chain, which makes up photosystem I. This system uses the energy released in electron transfer to join a proton to nicotinamide adenine dinucleotide phosphate (NADP+), a phosphorylated derivative of NAD+, forming NADPH. NADPH is a high-energy electron donor that, with ATP, fuels the conversion of carbon dioxide into the carbohydrate foods of the plant cell.

NADPH remains within the stroma of the chloroplast for use in the fixation of carbon dioxide (CO_2) during the Calvin cycle. In a complex cycle of chemical reactions, CO_2 is bound to a five-carbon ribulose biphosphate compound. The resulting six-carbon intermediate is then split into three-carbon phosphoglycerate. With energy supplied by the breakdown of NADPH and ATP, this compound is eventually formed into glyceraldehyde 3-phosphate, an important sugar intermediate of metabolism. One glyceraldehyde molecule is exported from the chloroplast, for further conversion in the cytoplasm, for every five that undergo an ATP-powered re-formation into the five-carbon ribulose biphosphate. In this way three molecules of CO_2 yield one molecule of glyceraldehyde 3-phosphate, while the entire fixation cycle hydrolyzes nine molecules of ATP and oxidizes six molecules of NADPH.

ENDOPLASMIC RETICULUM

The endoplasmic reticulum (ER) is a system of membranous cisternae (flattened sacs) extending throughout the cytoplasm. Often it constitutes more than half of the total membrane in the cell. This structure was first noted in the late 19th century, when studies of stained cells indicated the presence of some type of extensive cytoplasmic structure, then known as the gastroplasm. The

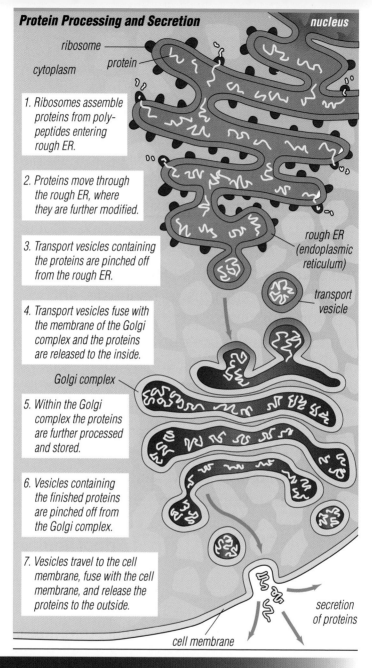

Protein Processing and Secretion

nucleus

ribosome

cytoplasm

protein

1. Ribosomes assemble proteins from polypeptides entering rough ER.

2. Proteins move through the rough ER, where they are further modified.

3. Transport vesicles containing the proteins are pinched off from the rough ER.

4. Transport vesicles fuse with the membrane of the Golgi complex and the proteins are released to the inside.

Golgi complex

5. Within the Golgi complex the proteins are further processed and stored.

6. Vesicles containing the finished proteins are pinched off from the Golgi complex.

7. Vesicles travel to the cell membrane, fuse with the cell membrane, and release the proteins to the outside.

rough ER (endoplasmic reticulum)

transport vesicle

secretion of proteins

cell membrane

The endoplasmic reticulum (ER) plays a major role in the biosynthesis of proteins. Proteins that are synthesized by ribosomes on the ER are transported into the Golgi apparatus for processing. Some of these proteins will be secreted from the cell, others will be inserted into the plasma membrane, and still others will be inserted into lysosomes.

electron microscope made possible the study of the morphology of this organelle in the 1940s, when it was given its present name.

The endoplasmic reticulum can be classified into two functionally distinct forms, the smooth endoplasmic reticulum (SER) and the rough endoplasmic reticulum (RER). The morphological distinction between the two is the presence of protein-synthesizing particles, called ribosomes, attached to the outer surface of the RER.

The functions of the SER, a meshwork of fine tubular membrane vesicles, vary considerably from cell to cell. One important role is the synthesis of phospholipids and cholesterol, which are major components of the plasma and internal membranes. Phospholipids are formed from fatty acids, glycerol phosphate, and other small water-soluble molecules by enzymes bound to the ER membrane with their active sites facing the cytosol. Some phospholipids remain in the ER membrane, where, catalyzed by specific enzymes within the membranes, they can "flip" from the cytoplasmic side of the bilayer, where they were formed, to the exoplasmic, or inner, side. This process ensures the symmetrical growth of the ER membrane. Other phospholipids are transferred through the cytoplasm to other membranous structures, such as the cell membrane and the mitochondrion, by special phospholipid transfer proteins.

In liver cells, the SER is specialized for the detoxification of a wide variety of compounds produced by metabolic processes. Liver SER contains a number of enzymes called cytochrome P450, which catalyze the breakdown of carcinogens and other organic molecules. In cells of the adrenal glands and gonads, cholesterol is modified in the SER at one stage of its conversion to steroid hormones. Finally, the SER in muscle cells, known as the sarcoplasmic reticulum, sequesters calcium ions from the cytoplasm. When the muscle is triggered by nerve stimuli, the calcium ions are released, causing muscle contraction.

The RER is generally a series of connected flattened sacs. It plays a central role in the synthesis and export of proteins and glycoproteins and is best studied in the secretory cells specialized in these functions. The many secretory cells in the human body include liver cells secreting serum proteins such as albumin, endocrine cells secreting peptide hormones such as insulin, salivary gland and pancreatic acinar cells secreting digestive enzymes, mammary gland cells secreting milk proteins, and cartilage cells secreting collagen and proteoglycans.

Ribosomes are particles that synthesize proteins from amino acids. They are composed of four RNA molecules and between 40 and 80 proteins assembled into a large and a small subunit. Ribosomes are either free (i.e., not bound to membranes) in the cytoplasm of the cell or bound to the RER.

Lysosomal enzymes, proteins destined for the ER, Golgi, and cell membranes, and proteins to be secreted from the cell are among those synthesized on membrane-bound ribosomes. Fabricated on free ribosomes are proteins remaining in the cytosol and those bound to the internal surface of the outer membrane, as well as those to be incorporated into the nucleus, mitochondria, chloroplasts, peroxisomes, and other organelles. Special features of proteins label them for transport to specific destinations inside or outside of the cell. In 1971 German-born cellular and molecular biologist Günter Blobel and Argentinian-born cellular biologist David Sabatini suggested that the amino-terminal portion of the protein (the first part of the molecule to be made) could act as a "signal sequence." They proposed that such a signal sequence would facilitate the attachment of the growing protein to the ER membrane and lead the protein either into the membrane or through the membrane into the ER lumen (interior).

The signal hypothesis has been substantiated by a large body of experimental evidence. Translation of the blueprint for a specific protein encoded in a messenger RNA molecule begins on a free ribosome. As the growing protein, with the signal sequence at its amino-terminal end, emerges from the ribosome, the sequence binds to a complex of six proteins and one RNA molecule known as the signal recognition particle (SRP). The SRP also binds to the ribosome to halt further formation of the protein. The membrane of the ER contains receptor sites that bind the SRP-ribosome complex to the RER membrane. Upon binding, translation resumes, with the SRP dissociating from the complex and the signal sequence and remainder of the nascent protein threading through the membrane, via a channel called a translocon, into the ER lumen. At that point, the protein is permanently segregated from the cytosol. In most cases, the signal sequence is cleaved from the protein by an enzyme called signal peptidase as it emerges on the luminal surface of the ER membrane. In addition, in a process known as glycosylation, oligosaccharide (complex sugar) chains are often added to the protein to form a glycoprotein. Inside the ER lumen, the protein folds into its characteristic three-dimensional conformation.

Within the lumen, proteins that will be secreted from the cell diffuse into the transitional portion of the ER, a region that is largely free of ribosomes. There the molecules are packaged into small membrane-bounded transport vesicles, which separate from the ER membrane and move through the cytoplasm to a target membrane, usually the Golgi complex. There the transport vesicle membrane fuses with the Golgi membrane, and the contents of the vesicle are delivered into the lumen of the Golgi. This, like all processes of vesicle budding and fusion, preserves the sidedness of the membranes. Thus, the cytoplasmic surface of the membrane always faces outward, and the luminal contents are always sequestered from the cytoplasm.

Certain nonsecretory proteins made on the RER remain part of the membrane system of the cell. These membrane proteins have, in addition to the signal sequence, one or more anchor regions composed of lipid-soluble amino acids. The amino acids prevent passage of the protein completely into the ER lumen by anchoring it into the phospholipid bilayer of the ER membrane.

GOLGI APPARATUS

The Golgi apparatus (also known as the Golgi complex, or Golgi body) is a membrane-bound organelle of eukaryotic cells that is made up of a series of flattened, stacked pouches called cisternae. The Golgi apparatus is responsible for transporting, modifying, and packaging proteins and lipids into vesicles for delivery to targeted destinations. It is located in the cytoplasm next to the endoplasmic reticulum and near the cell nucleus. While many types of cells contain only one or several Golgi apparatus, plant cells can contain hundreds.

In general, the Golgi apparatus is made up of approximately four to eight cisternae, although in some single-celled organisms it may consist of as many as 60 cisternae. The cisternae are held together

DISCOVERING THE GOLGI CELL AND GOLGI APPARATUS

Italian physician and cytologist Camillo Golgi (1843/44–1926) is known for his investigations into the fine structure of the nervous system, which earned him (with the Spanish histologist Santiago Ramón y Cajal) the 1906 Nobel Prize for Physiology or Medicine.

As a physician at a home for incurables in Abbiategrasso, Italy (1872–75), and with only rudimentary facilities at his disposal, Golgi devised (1873) the silver nitrate method of staining nerve tissue, an invaluable tool in subsequent nerve studies. This stain enabled him to demonstrate the existence of a kind of nerve cell (which came to be known as the Golgi cell) possessing many short, branching extensions (dendrites) and serving to connect several other nerve cells. The discovery of Golgi cells led German anatomist Wilhelm von Waldeyer Hartz to postulate, and Ramón y Cajal to establish, that the nerve cell is the basic structural unit of the nervous system, a critical point in the development of modern neurology.

After his arrival at the University of Pavia (1875), Golgi found and described (1880) the point (now known as the Golgi tendon spindle or Golgi tendon organ) at which sensory nerve fibres end in rich branchings encapsulated within a tendon. He also discovered (1883) the presence in nerve cells of an irregular network of fibrils (small fibres), vesicles (cavities), and granules, now known as the Golgi apparatus. The Golgi apparatus is found in all eukaryotic cells and plays an important role in the modification and transport of proteins within the cell.

Turning to the study of malaria (1885–93), Golgi found that the two types of intermittent malarial fevers (tertian, occurring every other day, and quartan, occurring every third day) are caused by different species of the protozoan parasite *Plasmodium* and that the paroxysms of fever coincide with release of the parasite's spores from red blood cells.

by matrix proteins, and the whole of the Golgi apparatus is supported by cytoplasmic microtubules. The apparatus has three primary compartments, known generally as cis (cisternae nearest the endoplasmic reticulum), medial (central layers of cisternae), and trans (cisternae farthest from the endoplasmic reticulum). Two networks, the cis Golgi network and the trans Golgi network, which are made up of the outermost cisternae at the cis and trans faces, are responsible for the essential task of sorting proteins and lipids that are received (at the cis face) or released (at the trans face) by the organelle.

The proteins and lipids received at the cis face arrive in clusters of fused vesicles. These fused vesicles migrate along microtubules through a special trafficking compartment, called the vesicular-tubular cluster, that lies between the endoplasmic reticulum and the Golgi apparatus. When a vesicle cluster fuses with the cis membrane, the contents are delivered into the lumen of the cis face cisterna. As proteins and lipids progress from the cis face to the trans face, they are modified into functional molecules and are marked for delivery to specific intracellular or extracellular locations. Some modifications involve cleavage of oligosaccharide side chains followed by attachment of different sugar portions in place of the side chain. Other modifications may involve the addition of fatty acids or phosphate groups (phosphorylation) or the removal of monosaccharides. The different enzyme-driven modification reactions are specific to the compartments of the Golgi apparatus. For example, the removal of mannose portions occurs primarily in the cis and medial cisternae, whereas the addition of galactose or sulfate occurs primarily in the trans cisternae. In the final stage of transport through the Golgi apparatus, modified proteins and lipids are sorted in the trans Golgi network and are packaged into vesicles at the trans face. These vesicles then deliver the molecules to their target destinations, such as lysosomes or the cell membrane. Some molecules, including certain soluble proteins and secretory proteins, are carried in vesicles to the cell membrane for exocytosis (release into the extracellular environment). The exocytosis of secretory proteins may be regulated, whereby a ligand must bind to a receptor to trigger vesicle fusion and protein secretion.

The way in which proteins and lipids move from the cis face to the trans face is of some debate, and today there exist two models, with quite different perceptions of the Golgi apparatus, competing to explain this movement. The vesicular transport model stems from initial studies that identified vesicles in association with the Golgi apparatus. This model is based on the idea that vesicles bud off and fuse to cisternae membranes, thus moving molecules from one cisterna to the next. Budding vesicles can also be used to transport molecules back to the endoplasmic reticulum. A vital element of this model is that the cisternae themselves are stationary. In contrast, the cisternal maturation model depicts the Golgi apparatus as a far more dynamic organelle than does the vesicular transport model. The cisternal maturation model indicates that cis cisternae move forward and mature into trans cisternae, with new cis cisternae forming from the fusion of vesicles at the cis face. In this model, vesicles are formed but are used only to transport molecules back to the endoplasmic reticulum.

The Golgi apparatus was observed in 1897 by Italian cytologist Camillo Golgi. In Golgi's early studies of nervous tissue, he had established a staining technique that he referred to as reazione nera, meaning "black reaction." Today this method is known as the Golgi stain. In this technique nervous tissue is fixed with potassium dichromate and then suffused with silver nitrate. While examining neurons that Golgi stained using his black reaction, he identified an "internal reticular apparatus." This structure became known as the Golgi apparatus, though some scientists questioned whether the structure was real and attributed the find to free-floating particles of Golgi's metal stain. In the 1950s, however, when the electron microscope came into use, the existence of the Golgi apparatus was confirmed.

SECRETORY VESICLES

The release of proteins or other molecules from a secretory vesicle is most often stimulated by a nervous or hormonal signal. For example, a nerve cell impulse triggers the fusion of secretory vesicles to the membrane at the nerve terminal, where the vesicles release neurotransmitters into the synaptic cleft (the gap between nerve endings). The action is one of exocytosis: The vesicle and the cell membrane fuse, allowing the proteins and glycoproteins in the vesicle to be released to the cell exterior.

As secretory vesicles fuse with the cell membrane, the area of the cell membrane increases. Normal size is regained by the reuptake of membrane components through endocytosis. Regions bud in from the cell membrane and then fuse with internal membranes to effect recycling.

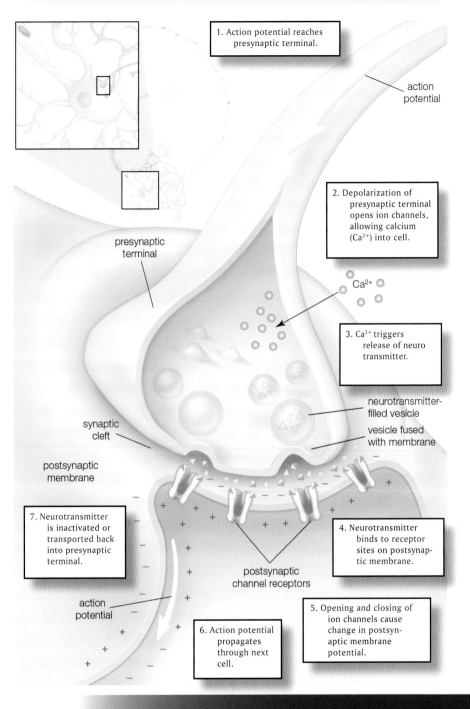

1. Action potential reaches presynaptic terminal.

action potential

2. Depolarization of presynaptic terminal opens ion channels, allowing calcium (Ca^{2+}) into cell.

presynaptic terminal

Ca^{2+}

3. Ca^{2+} triggers release of neuro transmitter.

neurotransmitter-filled vesicle

vesicle fused with membrane

synaptic cleft

postsynaptic membrane

7. Neurotransmitter is inactivated or transported back into presynaptic terminal.

4. Neurotransmitter binds to receptor sites on postsynaptic membrane.

postsynaptic channel receptors

action potential

5. Opening and closing of ion channels cause change in postsynaptic membrane potential.

6. Action potential propagates through next cell.

The arrival of the nerve impulse at the presynaptic terminal stimulates the release of neurotransmitters into the synaptic gap. The binding of the neurotransmitter to receptors on the postsynaptic membrane stimulates the regeneration of the action potential in the postsynaptic neuron.

LYSOSOMES

Lysosomes are subcellular organelles that are found in all eukaryotic cells. They are responsible for cellular digestion of macromolecules, old cell parts, and microorganisms. Each lysosome is surrounded by a membrane that maintains an acidic environment within the interior via a proton pump. Lysosomes contain a wide variety of hydrolytic enzymes (acid hydrolases) that break down macromolecules such as nucleic acids, proteins, and polysaccharides. These enzymes are active only in the lysosome's acidic interior. Their acid-dependent activity protects the cell from self-degradation in case of lysosomal leakage or rupture, since the pH of the cell is neutral to slightly alkaline. Lysosomes were discovered by Belgian cytologist Christian René de Duve in the 1950s.

Lysosomes originate by budding off from the membrane of the trans-Golgi network. The lysosomes then fuse with membrane vesicles that derive from one of three pathways: endocytosis, autophagocytosis, and phagocytosis. In endocytosis, extracellular macromolecules are taken up into the cell to form membrane-bound vesicles called endosomes that fuse with lysosomes. Autophagocytosis is the process by which old organelles are removed from a cell. They are enveloped by internal membranes that then fuse with lysosomes. Phago-

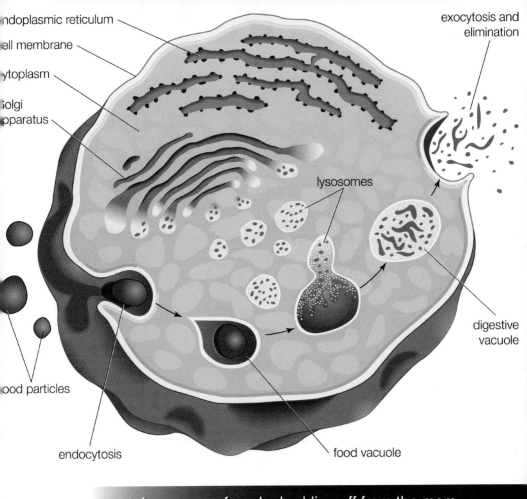

endoplasmic reticulum

cell membrane

cytoplasm

Golgi apparatus

exocytosis and elimination

lysosomes

digestive vacuole

food particles

endocytosis

food vacuole

Lysosomes form by budding off from the membrane of the trans-Golgi network. Macromolecules (i.e., food particles) are absorbed into the cell in vesicles formed by endocytosis. The vesicles fuse with lysosomes, which then break down the macromolecules using hydrolytic enzymes.

cytosis is carried out by specialized cells (e.g., macrophages) that engulf large extracellular particles such as dead cells or foreign invaders (e.g., bacteria) and target them for lysosomal degradation. Many of

RESEARCH ON AUTOPHAGY

Japanese cell biologist Yoshinori Ohsumi (1945–), who won the 2016 Nobel Prize for Physiology or Medicine, is known for his work in elucidating the mechanisms of autophagy, a process by which cells degrade and recycle proteins and other cellular components. Ohsumi's research played a key role in helping to uncover the critical physiological activities of autophagy, including its function in helping cells adapt to various types of stress, in contributing to embryo development, and in eliminating damaged proteins.

Beginning in 1988 Ohsumi studied vacuoles (membrane-bound fluid-filled organelles), focusing in particular on the lytic (degradation) activities of vacuoles in yeast, about which very little was known at the time. Drastic cellular degradation processes, known as autophagy, or "self-eating," had been described and studied extensively in animal cells, however, providing Ohsumi with a basis for investigation. Of particular significance was the observation that in animal cells, autophagy could be induced by exposing the cells to nutrient-deficient conditions. In a parallel experiment, Ohsumi engineered the yeast *Saccharomyces cerevisiae* to lack vacuolar protein-ase and peptidase enzymes (thereby preventing sporulation) and then deprived the yeast cells of nutrients. When he observed the yeast under a light microscope, he found that autophagic bodies had accumulated inside the vacuoles. He published the findings—the first to demonstrate the existence of autophagy in yeast—in 1992.

Shortly thereafter Ohsumi used his engineered yeast to identify genes essential to autophagy. Researchers working in his laboratory eventually found and characterized the function of 14 autophagy genes in yeast. They subsequently found that enzymes encoded by some of the genes were conjugated (joined together), providing evidence of a complete autophagic pathway in yeast. Moreover, several of the genes were homologous to mammalian genes, suggesting the existence of a corresponding pathway in human cells. In later research Ohsumi elucidated the mechanism of formation of the autophagosome (in animal cells, the vesicle that engulfs cellular components and delivers them to the lysosome, where they undergo degradation) and the role of stress in initiating autophagy.

Ohsumi's work proved critical in explaining the mechanism by which cells eliminate worn-out protein complexes and organelles, which are otherwise too large to be degraded by other means. The abnormal accumulation of such components is highly damaging to cells and is known to play a role in certain diseases. Thus, Ohsumi's findings had significant implications for the understanding and treatment of various conditions in which autophagy is disrupted, including cancer, Parkinson disease, and type 2 diabetes mellitus.

the products of lysosomal digestion, such as amino acids and nucleotides, are recycled back to the cell for use in the synthesis of new cellular components.

Lysosomal storage diseases are genetic disorders in which a genetic mutation affects the activity of one or more of the acid hydrolases. In such diseases, the normal metabolism of specific macromolecules is blocked and the macromolecules accumulate inside the lysosomes, causing severe physiological damage or deformity. Hurler syndrome, which involves a defect in the metabolism of mucopolysaccharides, is a lysosomal storage disease.

MICROBODIES AND PEROXISOMES

Microbodies are roughly spherical in shape, bound by a single membrane, and are usually 0.5 to 1 micrometre in diameter. There are several types, by far the most common of which is the peroxisome.

Peroxisomes containenzymes thatoxidize certain molecules normally found in the cell, notably fatty acids and amino acids. These oxidation reactions produce hydrogen peroxide, which is the basis of the name peroxisome.

However, hydrogen peroxide is potentially toxic to the cell, because it has the ability to react with many other molecules. Therefore, peroxisomes also contain enzymes such as catalase that convert hydrogen peroxide to water and oxygen, thereby neutralizing the toxicity. In this way peroxisomes provide a safe location for the oxidative metabolism of certain molecules. The plant glyoxysome is a peroxisome that also contains the enzymes of the glyoxylate cycle, which is crucial to the conversion of fat into carbohydrate.

Peroxisomes have a special transporter system for taking up their enzymes from the cytoplasm. Mutations in genes that encode the enzymes and transporter proteins of the peroxisome are responsible for a number of human diseases, including Zellweger syndrome, a congenital disorder characterized by complete absence or reduction in number of peroxisomes. Mutations giving rise to this syndrome cause copper, iron, and substances called very long chain fatty acids to accumulate in the blood and in tissues, such as the liver, brain, and kidneys. Infants with Zellweger syndrome are often born with facial deformity and intellectual disability. Some affected infants may have impaired vision and hearing and may experience severe gastrointestinal bleeding or liver failure. Prognosis is poor—most infants with this syndrome do not live beyond one year.

Peroxisomes were identified and described in the 1950s as part of the pioneering work of Christian René de Duve, who developed cell fractionation techniques. De Duve's method separated organelles based on their sedimentation and density properties. Because peroxisomes are denser than other organelles, de Duve was able to isolate and characterize them relatively easily. De Duve shared the 1974 Nobel Prize for Physiology or Medicine with Albert Claude and George Palade for this work.

VACUOLES

Most plant cells contain one or more membrane-bound vesicles called vacuoles. Within the vacuole is the cell sap, a water solution of salts and sugars kept at high concentration by the active transport of ions through permeases in the vacuole membrane. Proton pumps also maintain high concentrations of protons in the vacuole interior. These high concentrations cause the entry, via osmosis, of water into the vacuole, which in turn expands the vacuole and generates a hydrostatic pressure, called turgor, that presses the cell membrane against the cell wall. Turgor is the cause of rigidity in living plant tissue. In the mature plant cell, as much as 90 percent of cell volume may be taken up by a single vacuole. Immature cells typically contain several smaller vacuoles.

CHAPTER
4

CELL COMMUNICATION

The development of single cells into multicellular organisms involves a number of adaptations. The cells become specialized, acquiring distinct functions that contribute to the survival of the organism. The behaviour of individual cells is also integrated with that of similar cells, so that they act together in a regulated fashion. To achieve this integration, cells assemble into specialized tissues, each tissue being composed of cells and the spaces outside of the cells. The surface of cells is important in coordinating their activities within tissues. Embedded in the plasma membrane of each cell are a number of proteins that interact with the surface or secretions of other cells. These proteins enable cells to "recognize" and adhere to the extracellular matrix and one another and to form populations distinct from surrounding cells. These interactions are key to

151

the organizational behaviour of cell populations and contribute to the formation of embryonic tissues and the function of normal tissue in the adult organism.

EXTRACELLULAR MATRIX

A substantial part of tissues is the space outside of the cells, called the extracellular space. This is filled with a composite material, known as the extracellular matrix, composed of a gel in which a number

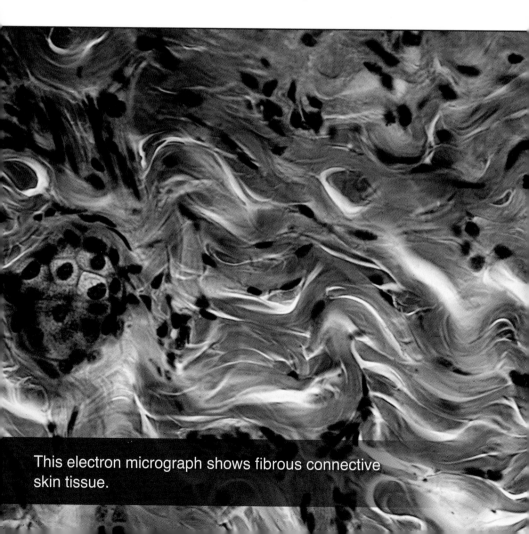

This electron micrograph shows fibrous connective skin tissue.

of fibrous proteins are suspended. The gel consists of large polysaccharide (complex sugar) molecules in a water solution of inorganic salts, nutrients, and waste products known as the interstitial fluid. The major types of protein in the matrix are structural proteins and adhesive proteins.

There are two general types of tissues distinct not only in their cellular organization but also in the composition of their extracellular matrix. The first type, mesenchymal tissue, is made up of clusters of cells grouped together but not closely adherent to one another. They synthesize a highly hydrated gel, rich in salts, fluid, and fibres, known as the interstitial matrix. Connective tissue is a mesenchyme that fastens together other more highly organized tissues. The solidity of various connective tissues varies according to the consistency of their extracellular matrix, which in turn depends on the water content of the gels, the amount and type of polysaccharides and structural proteins, and the presence of other salts. For example, bone is rich in calcium phosphate, giving that tissue its rigidity, and tendons are mostly fibrous structural proteins, yielding a ropelike consistency. Joint spaces are filled with a lubricating fluid of mostly polysaccharide and interstitial fluid.

Epithelial tissues, the second type, are sheets of cells adhering at their side, or lateral, surfaces. They synthesize and deposit at their bottom, or basal, surfaces an organized complex of matrix materials known as the basal lamina or basement membrane. This thin layer serves as a boundary with connective tissue and as a substrate to which epithelial cells are attached.

MATRIX POLYSACCHARIDES

The polysaccharides, or glycans, of the extracellular matrix are responsible for its gel-like quality and for organizing its components. These large acidic molecules exist alone (as glycosaminoglycans) or in combination with small proteins (as proteoglycans). They bind an extraordinarily large amount of water, thus forming massively swollen gels that fill the spaces between cells. Bound to proteins, they also organize other molecules in the extracellular matrix. The firmness and resiliency of cartilage, as at the surface of joints, is due to highly organized proteoglycans that bind water tightly.

MATRIX PROTEINS

Matrix proteins are large molecules tightly bound to form extensive networks of insoluble fibres. These fibres may even exceed the size of the cells themselves. The proteins are of two general types, structural and adhesive. The structural proteins, collagen and elastin, are the dominant matrix proteins. At least 10 different types of collagen are present in various tissues. The most common, type I collagen, is the most abundant protein in vertebrate animals, accounting for nearly 25 percent of the total protein in the body. The various collagen types share structural features, all being composed of three intertwined polypeptide chains. In some collagens the chains are linked together by covalent bonds, yielding a ropelike structure of great tensile strength. Indeed, the toughness of leather, chemically treated animal skin, is due to its content of collagen. Elastin is also a cross-linked protein, but, instead of forming rigid coils, it imparts elasticity to tissues. Only one type of elastin is known. It varies in elasticity according to variations in its cross-linking.

The adhesive proteins of the extracellular matrix bind matrix molecules to one another and to cell surfaces. These proteins are modular in that they contain several functional domains packaged together in a single molecule. Each domain binds to a specific matrix component or to a specific site on a cell. The major adhesive protein of the interstitial matrix is called fibronectin, and the equivalent protein in the basal lamina is known as laminin.

CELL-MATRIX INTERACTIONS

Molecules intimately associated with the cell membrane link cells to the extracellular matrix. These molecules, called matrix receptors, bind selectively to specific matrix of components and interact, directly or indirectly, with actin protein fibres that form the cytoskeleton inside the cell. This association of actin fibres with matrix components via receptors on the cell membrane can influence the organization of membrane molecules as well as matrix components and can modify the shape and function of the cyto-skeleton. Changes in the cytoskeleton can lead to changes in cell shape, movement, metabolism, and development.

CYTOSKELETON

The cytoskeleton is the name given to the fibrous network formed by different types of long protein filaments present throughout the cytoplasm of eukaryotic cells. The filaments of the cytoskeleton create a scaffold, or framework, that organizes other cell constituents and maintains the shape of the cell. In addition, some filaments cause coherent move-ments, both of the cell itself and of its internal organ-elles. Prokaryotic cells contain a unique related set of filaments but, with few exceptions, do not possess true cytoskeletons. Their shapes and the shapes of certain eukaryotes, primarily yeast and other fungi, are determined by the rigid cell wall on the outside of the cell.

Four major types of cytoskeletal filaments are commonly recognized: actin filaments, microtubules, intermediate filaments, and septins. Actin filaments and microtubules are dynamic structures that continuously assemble and disassemble in most cells. Intermediate filaments are stabler and seem to be involved mainly in reinforcing cell structures, especially the position of the nucleus and the junctions that connect cells. Septins are involved in cell division and have been implicated in other cell functions. A wide variety of accessory proteins works in concert with each type of filament, linking filaments to one another and to the cell membrane and helping to form the networks that endow the cytoskeleton with its unique functions. Many of these accessory proteins have been characterized, revealing a rich diversity in the structure and function of the cytoskeleton.

ACTIN FILAMENTS

Actin is a globular protein that polymerizes (joins together many small molecules) to form long filaments. Because each actin subunit faces in the same direction, the actin filament is polar, with different ends, termed "barbed" and "pointed." An abundant protein in nearly all eukaryotic cells, actin has been extensively studied in muscle cells. In muscle cells, the actin filaments are organized into regular arrays that are complementary with a set of thicker filaments formed from a second protein called myosin.

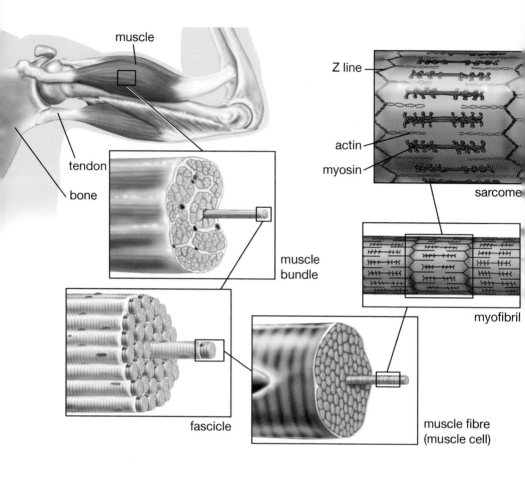

muscle

Z line

actin

myosin

sarcome

myofibril

muscle
bundle

tendon

bone

fascicle

muscle fibre
(muscle cell)

Striated muscle tissue, such as the tissue of the human biceps muscle, consists of long, fine fibres, each of which is in effect a bundle of finer myofibrils. Within each myofibril are filaments of the proteins myosin and actin; these filaments slide past one another as the muscle contracts and expands. On each myofibril, regularly occurring dark bands, called Z lines, can be seen where actin and myosin filaments overlap. The region between two Z lines is called a sarcomere; sarcomeres can be considered the primary structural and functional unit of muscle tissue.

These two proteins create the force responsible for muscle contraction.

When the signal to contract is sent along a nerve to the muscle, the actin and myosin are activated. Myosin works as a motor, hydrolyzing ATP to release energy in such a way that a myosin filament moves along an actin filament, causing the two filaments to slide past each other. The thin actin filaments and the thick myosin filaments are organized in a structure called the sarcomere, which shortens as the filaments slide over one another. Skeletal muscles are composed of bundles of many long muscle cells. When the sarcomeres contract, each of these giant muscle cells shortens, and the overall effect is the contraction of the entire muscle. Although the stimulation pathways differ, heart muscle and smooth muscle (found in many internal organs and blood vessels) contract by a similar sliding filament mechanism.

Actin is also present in non-muscle cells, where it forms a meshwork of filaments responsible for many types of cellular movement. The meshwork consists of actin filaments that are attached to the cell membrane and to each other. The length of the filaments and the architecture of their attachments determine the shape and consistency of a cell. A large number of accessory proteins bind to actin, controlling the number, length, position, and attachments of the actin filaments. Different cells and tissues contain different accessory proteins, which accounts for the different shapes and movements of different cells. For example, in some cells, actin filaments are bundled by accessory proteins, and the bundle is attached to the cell membrane to form microvilli, stable protrusions that resemble tiny bristles. Microvilli on the surface of epithelial cells, such as those lining the intestine, increase the cell's surface area and thus facilitate the absorption of ingested food and water molecules. Other types of microvilli are involved in the detection of sound in the ear, where their movement, caused by sound waves, sends an electrical signal to the brain.

Many actin filaments in non-muscle cells have only a transient existence, polymerizing and depolymerizing in controlled ways that create movement. For example, many cells continually send out and retract tiny filopodia, long needle like projections of the cell membrane that are thought to enable cells to probe their environment and decide which direction to go. Like microvilli, filopodia are formed when actin filaments push out the membrane, but, because these actin filaments are less stable, filopodia have only a brief existence. Another actin structure only transiently associated with the cell membrane is the contractile ring, which is composed of actin filaments running around the circumference of the cell during cell division. As its name implies, this ring pulls in the cell membrane by a myosin-dependent process, thereby pinching the cell in half.

MICROTUBULES

Microtubules are long filaments formed from 13 to 15 protofilament strands of a globular subunit called tubulin, with the strands arranged in the form of a hollow cylinder. Like actin filaments, microtubules are polar, having plus and minus ends. Most microtubule plus ends are constantly growing and shrinking, by respectively adding and losing subunits at their ends. Stable microtubules are found in cilia and flagella. Cilia are hairlike structures found on the surface of certain types of epithelial cells, where they beat in unison to move fluid and particles over the cell surface. Cilia are closely related in structure to flagella. Flagella, such as those found on sperm cells, produce a helical wavelike motion that enables a cell to propel itself rapidly through fluids. In cilia and flagella a set of microtubules is connected in a regular array by numerous accessory proteins that act as links and spokes in the assembly. Movement of the cilia or flagella occurs when adjacent microtubules slide past one another, bending the structures. This motion is caused by the motor protein dynein, which uses the energy of ATP hydrolysis to move along the microtubules, in a manner resembling the movement of myosin along actin filaments.

In most cells, microtubules grow outward, from the cell centre to the cell membrane, from a special region of the cytoplasm near the nuclear envelope called the centrosome. The minus ends of these microtubules are embedded in the centrosome, while the plus ends terminate near the cell membrane. The plus ends grow and shrink rapidly, a process known as dynamic instability. At the start of cell division, the centrosome replicates and divides in two. The two centrosomes separate and move to opposite sides of the nuclear envelope, where each nucleates a star like array of microtubules, forming the mitotic spindle. The mitotic spindle partitions the duplicated chromosomes into the two daughter cells during mitosis.

Microtubules often serve as tracks for the transport of membrane vesicles in the cell, carried by the motor proteins kinesin and dynein. Kinesins generally move toward the plus end of the microtubule, and dyneins move toward the minus end. Microtubule-based vesicle transport occurs in nearly all cells, but it is especially prominent in the long thin processes of neurons, carrying essential components to and from the synapses at the ends of the processes.

INTERMEDIATE FILAMENTS

Intermediate filaments are so named because they are thicker than actin filaments and thinner than microtubules or muscle myosin filaments. The sub-units of intermediate filaments are elongated, not globular, and are associated in an antipolar manner. As a result, the overall filament has no polarity, and therefore no motor proteins move along interme-diate filaments. Intermediate filaments are found only in complex multicellular organisms. They are encoded by a large number of different genes and can be grouped into families based on their amino acid sequences. Cells in different tissues of the body express one or another of these genes at dif-ferent times. One cell can even change which type of intermediate filament protein is expressed over its lifetime. Most likely, the different forms of interme-diate filaments have subtle but critical differences in their functional characteristics, helping to define the function of the cell. In general, intermediate fil-aments serve as structural elements, helping cells maintain their shape and integrity. For example, ker-atin filaments, the intermediate filaments of epithelial cells, which line surfaces of the body, give strength to the cell sheet that covers the surface. Mutations in keratin genes can result in blisters when the epi-thelial cell sheet is weak and prone to rupture. Ker-atin mutations can also cause deformations in the hair, nails, and corneas. Another example of a family of intermediate filaments is the lamin family, which comprises the nuclear lamina, a fibrous shell that underlies and supports the nuclear membrane.

RECOGNITION AND ADHESION

The ability of cells to recognize and adhere to one another plays an important role in cell survival and reproduction. For example, when starved, several types of single-cell organisms band together to develop the specialized cells needed for reproduction. In this process, certain cells at the centre of the developing aggregate secrete chemicals that cause the other cells to adhere tightly into a group. In the case of slime mold amoebas, starvation causes the secretion of a compound, cyclic adenosine monophosphate (cyclic AMP, or cAMP), that induces the cells to stick together end to end. With further aggregation, the cells produce another cell-surface glycoprotein with which they stick to one another over their entire surfaces. The cellular aggregates then produce an extracellular matrix, which holds the cells together in a specific structural form.

TISSUE AND SPECIES RECOGNITION

Some multicellular animals or tissues can be dissociated into suspensions of single cells that show the same cellular recognition and adhesion as do aggregates of single-cell organisms. The marine sponge, for example, can be sieved through a mesh, yielding single cells and cells in clumps.

When this cell suspension is rotated in culture, the cells reaggregate and in time reform a normal sponge. This reassociation shows selective cell recognition—only cells of the same species reassociate. The ability of the cells to distinguish cells of their own species from those of others is mediated by proteoglycan molecules in the extracellular matrix. The proteoglycan binds to specific cell-surface receptor sites that are unique to a single species of sponge.

Cells from tissues of vertebrate animals can, like sponge cells, be dissociated and allowed to reaggregate. For example, when vertebrate embryonic cells from two different tissues are dissociated and then rotated together in culture, the cells form a multicellular aggregate within which they sort according to the type of tissue, a sorting that occurs regardless of whether the cells are from the same or different species. The specificity is due to a set of cell-surface glycoproteins called cell adhesion molecules (CAM). A portion of the CAM that extends from the surface of a cell adheres to identical molecules on the surface of adjacent cells. These CAM appear early in embryonic life, and their amounts in tissues change as the organs develop. The CAM, however, are not responsible for the stable adhesion of one cell to another. Such sturdier forms of adhesion are carried out by cell junctions.

CELL JUNCTIONS

There are three functional categories of cell junction: adhering junctions, often called desmosomes; tight, or occluding, junctions; and gap, or permeable, junctions. Adhering junctions hold cells together mechanically and are associated with intracellular fibres of the intercellular seal by fusion of adjacent cell membranes. Both adhering junctions and tight junctions are present primarily in epithelial cells. Many cell types also possess gap junctions, which allow small molecules to pass from one cell to the next through a channel.

ADHERING JUNCTIONS

Cells subject to abrasion or other mechanical stress, such as those of the surface epithelia of the skin, have junctions that adhere cells to one another and to the extracellular matrix. These adhering junctions are called desmosomes when occurring between cells and hemidesmosomes (half-desmosomes) when linked to the matrix. Adhering junctions distribute mechanical shear force throughout the tissue and to the underlying matrix by virtue of their association with intermediate filaments crossing the interior of the cell. The linkage of these filaments, also called keratin filaments, to the desmosomes and, through these junctions, to adjacent cells provides a nearly continuous fibrous network throughout an epithelial sheet. Adhering junctions are also seen in other types of cells—for example, in the muscles of the heart and uterus—allowing these cells to remain anchored together despite the contractions of the muscles.

TIGHT JUNCTIONS

Sheets of cells separate fluids within the organs from fluids outside, as in the epithelial layer lining the intestine. This separation requires leakproof junctions between cells. Tight junctions form leakproof seals by fusing the plasma membranes of adjacent cells, creating a continuous barrier through which molecules cannot pass. The membranes are fused by tight associations of two types of specialized integral membrane proteins, in turn repelling large water-soluble molecules. In invertebrates this function is provided by separate junctions, in which the proteins of the membrane, rather than the lipids, form the seal.

GAP JUNCTIONS

These junctions allow communication between adjacent cells via the passage of small molecules directly from the cytoplasm of one cell to that of another. Molecules that can pass between cells coupled by gap junctions include inorganic salts, sugars, amino acids, nucleotides, and vitamins but not large molecules such as proteins or nucleic acids.

Gap junctions are crucial to the integration of certain cellular activities. For example, heart muscle cells generate electrical current by the movement of inorganic salts. If the cells are coupled, they will share this electrical current, allowing the synchronous contraction of all the cells in the tissue. This coupling function requires the regulation of molecular traffic through the gaps. The junctions are not open pores but dynamic channels, which change their permeability with changes in cellular activity. They consist of proteins completely crossing the cell membrane as six-sided columns with central pores. Under certain conditions the proteins are thought to change shape, causing the pores to become smaller or larger and thus changing the permeability of the junction.

Gap junctions are also found in tissues that are not electrically active. In these tissues, the junctions allow nutrients and waste products to travel throughout the tissue. Cells in such tissues are said to be metabolically coupled. During the formation of embryos, gap junctions are crucial to establishing differences between separate groups of cells, the coupled cells undergoing development together to become a specialized tissue.

CHEMICAL SIGNALING

In addition to cell-matrix and cell-cell interactions, cell behaviour in multicellular organisms is coordinated by the passage of chemical or electrical signals between cells. The most common form of chemical signaling is via molecules secreted from the cells and moving through the extracellular space. Signaling molecules may also remain on cell surfaces, influencing other cells only after the cells make physical contact. Finally, as noted previously, gap junctions allow small molecules to move between the cytoplasms of adjacent cells.

Chemical signals secreted by cells can act over varying distances. In the autocrine signaling process, molecules act on the same cells that produce them. In paracrine signaling, they act on nearby cells. Autocrine signals include extracellular matrix molecules and various factors that stimulate cell growth. An example of paracrine signals is the chemical transmitted from nerve to muscle that causes the muscle to contract. In this instance, the muscle cells have regions specialized to receive chemical signals from an adjacent nerve cell. In both autocrine and paracrine signaling, the chemical signal works in the immediate vicinity of the cell that produces it and is present at high concentrations. A chemical signal picked up by the bloodstream and taken to distant sites is called an endocrine signal. Most hormones produced in vertebrates are endocrine signals, such as the hormones produced in the pituitary gland at the base of the brain and carried by the bloodstream to act at low concentrations on the thyroid or adrenal glands.

The concentration at which a chemical signal acts has significance for its target cell. Chemical signals that act at high concentration act locally and rapidly. Conversely, chemical signals that act at low concentrations act at distances and are generally slow.

SIGNAL RECEPTORS

The ability of a cell to respond to an extracellular signal depends on the presence of specific proteins called receptors, which are located on the cell surface or in the cytoplasm. Receptor molecules receive signals for a cell. Small molecules, such as hormones outside the cell or second messengers inside the cell, bind tightly and specifically to their receptors. Binding is a critical element in effecting a cellular response to a signal and is influenced by a cell's ability to express only certain receptor genes.

Molecules that bind to receptors, called ligands, can function as agonists, which stimulate the receptor to transmit signal information, or as antagonists, which inhibit, or prevent, the receptor from transmitting information. Antagonists can compete with agonists and thereby block an agonist's action. As

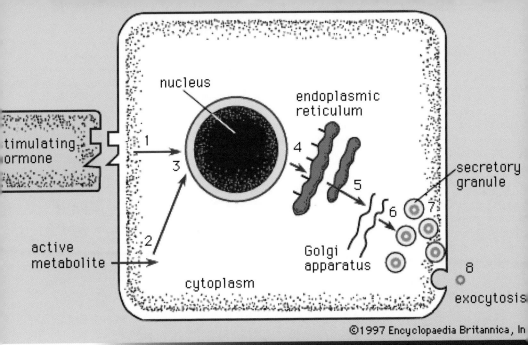

nucleus

endoplasmic reticulum

stimulating hormone

active metabolite

cytoplasm

Golgi apparatus

secretory granule

exocytosis

1

2

3

4

5

6

7

8

©1997 Encyclopaedia Britannica, In

Hormones and active metabolites bind to different types of receptors. Water-soluble molecules (e.g., insulin) cannot pass through the lipid membrane of a cell and thus rely on cell surface receptors to transmit messages to the interior of the cell. In contrast, lipid-soluble molecules (e.g., certain active metabolites) are able to diffuse through the lipid membrane to communicate messages directly to the nucleus.

therapeutic agents, both agonists and antagonists have been useful. For example, the hormone adrenaline (epinephrine) increases blood pressure by activating beta-adrenergic receptors, which causes blood vessels to constrict. In contrast, antagonists called beta-blockers can be used as drugs to lower blood pressure because they inhibit the receptors, which allows blood vessels to relax.

Cells can use similar receptors for remarkably divergent activities. For example, H1-type histamine receptors in the airways contribute to allergy symptoms, whereas H2-type receptors in the stomach promote the secretion of acid. In both cases, agents that specifically block the receptors have been useful therapies.

Many different individual receptor molecules exist, and they can be expressed in a countless variety of patterns. Receptor expression is critical in determining how organisms interact with their environment. The sense of smell (olfaction) is based on small molecules in the air (odorants) binding to receptor molecules on the surface of cells in the nose. The human genome contains roughly 1,000 genes for olfactory-type receptors, which are expressed in olfactory sensory neurons. Although many of these genes are inactive, this number is remarkably large, comprising about 3 percent of the total number of genes and revealing the importance of smell for fitness in evolution. Linda Buck and Richard Axel won the Nobel Prize for Physiology or Medicine in 2004 for their research on olfactory receptors.

While many receptors sit at the cell membrane, exposing an outer surface to bind molecules that cannot penetrate the cell, other receptors are located inside the cell and bind to hormones that pass through the cell membrane. Receptors for steroid hormones (e.g., estrogen) are among the latter

DISCOVERING OLFACTORY RECEPTORS

American scientists Linda B. Buck (1947–) and Richard Axel (1946–) received the Nobel Prize for Physiology or Medicine in 2004 for discoveries concerning the olfactory system.

Buck first worked with Axel in the early 1980s at Columbia University in New York City, where Axel was a professor and Buck was his postdoctoral student. They later worked together at the Howard Hughes Medical Institute (HHMI).

In 1991 Buck and Axel jointly published a landmark scientific paper, based on research they had conducted with laboratory rats, that detailed their discovery of the family of 1,000 genes that encode, or produce, an equivalent number of olfactory receptors. These receptors are proteins responsible for detecting the odorant molecules in the air and are located on olfactory receptor cells, which are clustered within a small area in the back of the nasal cavity. The two scientists then clarified how the olfactory system functions by showing that each receptor cell has only one type of odour receptor, which is specialized to recognize a few odours. After odorant molecules bind to receptors, the receptor cells send electrical signals to the olfactory bulb in the brain. The brain combines information from several types of receptors in specific patterns, which are experienced as distinct odours.

Axel and Buck later determined that most of the details they uncovered about the sense of smell are

(Continued on the next page)

(Continued from the previous page)

virtually identical in rats, humans, and other animals, although they discovered that humans have only about 350 types of working olfactory receptors, about one-third the number in rats. Nevertheless, the genes that encode olfactory receptors in humans account for about 3 percent of all human genes. The work helped boost scientific interest in the possible existence of human pheromones, odorant molecules known to trigger sexual activity and certain other behaviour in many animals. Buck's HHMI laboratory carried on research into how odour perceptions are translated into emotional responses and instinctive behaviour. Axel's HHMI laboratory also studied how sensory information is represented and sought to create a topographic map of olfactory representation in the brain.

group. In some types of breast cancer, the cancer cells are stimulated to grow by the action of estrogen. In these cases, the anticancer agent tamoxifen can be effective because it binds to the receptor. However, in some types of breast cancer, the cells no longer express estrogen receptors, and tamoxifen is ineffective in these individuals. Therefore, determining the "receptor status" of the cells in a breast cancer is a key element of the diagnosis. Receptor status may also influence diagnosis and treatment of certain other types of human diseases such as Alzheimer disease.

Scientists are developing drug candidates that can destroy cancerous tumours without harming non-cancerous cells. Such research is usually tested on mice or other animals before a human clinical trial is conducted.

G PROTEIN-COUPLED RECEPTORS

G protein-coupled receptors (GPCR; also called seven transmembrane receptors, or heptahelical receptors) are located in the cell membrane. They bind extracellular substances and transmit signals from these substances to an intracellular molecule called a G protein (guanine nucleotide-binding protein). GPCRs are found in the cell membranes of a wide range of organisms, including mammals, plants, microorganisms, and invertebrates. There are numerous different types of GPCRs—some 1,000

Epinephrine-stimulated cAMP synthesis

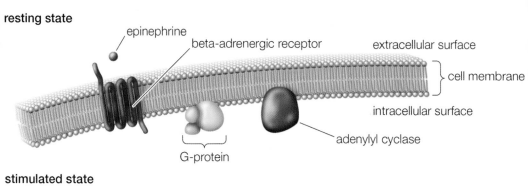

resting state

epinephrine

beta-adrenergic receptor

extracellular surface

cell membrane

intracellular surface

adenylyl cyclase

G-protein

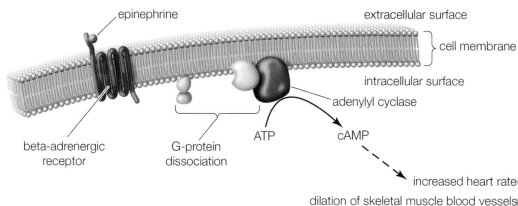

stimulated state

epinephrine

extracellular surface

cell membrane

intracellular surface

adenylyl cyclase

ATP

cAMP

beta-adrenergic receptor

G-protein dissociation

increased heart rate

dilation of skeletal muscle blood vessels

breakdown of glycogen to glucose

Epinephrine binds to a type of G protein-coupled receptor known as a beta-adrenergic receptor. When stimulated by epinephrine, this receptor activates a G protein that subsequently activates production of a molecule called cAMP (cyclic adenosine monophosphate). This results in the stimulation of cell-signaling pathways that act to increase heart rate, to dilate blood vessels in skeletal muscle, and to break down glycogen to glucose in the liver.

types are encoded by the human genome alone—and as a group they respond to a diverse range of substances, including light, hormones, amines, neurotransmitters, and lipids. Some examples of GPCRs include beta-adrenergic receptors, which bind epinephrine; prostaglandin E2 receptors, which bind inflammatory substances called prostaglandins; and rhodopsin, which contains a photoreactive chemical called retinal that responds to light signals received by rod cells in the eye.

A GPCR is made up of a long protein that has three basic regions: an extracellular portion (the N-terminus), an intracellular portion (the C-terminus), and a middle segment containing seven transmembrane domains. Beginning at the N-terminus, this long protein winds up and down through the cell membrane, with the long middle segment traversing the membrane seven times in a serpentine pattern. The last of the seven domains is connected to the C-terminus. When a GPCR binds a ligand, the ligand triggers a conformational change in the seven transmembrane region of the receptor. This activates the C-terminus, which then recruits a substance that in turn activates the G protein associated with the GPCR. Activation of the G protein initiates a series of intracellular reactions that end ultimately in the generation of some effect, such as increased heart rate in response to epinephrine or changes in vision in response to dim light.

RESEARCH ON GPCRS

American physicians and molecular biologists Robert J. Lefkowitz (1943–) and Brian K. Kobilka (1955–) shared the 2012 Nobel Prize for Chemistry for their research on the structure and function of cell-surface molecules known as G protein-coupled receptors (GPCRs), the largest family of signal-receiving molecules found in organisms. Their work revolutionized scientists' understanding of how cells respond to stimuli such as hormones and how certain types of drugs exert their actions, leading to major advances in drug development.

By 1970 Lefkowitz had successfully developed a procedure by which radioactively labeled adrenocorticotropic hormone (ACTH) would bind specifically to the membranes of cancer cells, and he had published evidence for the existence of cell-surface receptors. That year he left NIAMD for a residency and training in cardiovascular disease at Massachusetts General Hospital in Boston. In 1972, while working in the laboratory of German American physician and researcher Edgar Haber, he published a report detailing his purification of beta-adrenergic receptor protein from heart muscle cells (cardiomyocytes) in dogs. The beta-adrenergic receptor would later become a model system for the study of GPCRs.

In 1973 Lefkowitz joined the faculty at the Duke University Medical Center in Durham, North Carolina, where he later found that adrenergic receptors transmit signals to an intracellular molecule called a G protein (guanine nucleotide-binding protein), which had been discovered earlier by American pharmacologist Alfred G. Gilman and American biochemist Martin Rodbell (who shared the 1994 Nobel Prize for Physiology or Medicine for their independent discovery of G proteins). When activated, G proteins stimulate an enzyme known as adenylate cyclase, which converts the energy-carrying molecule ATP (adenosine triphosphate) to cAMP (cyclic adenosine monophosphate), a process responsible for producing physiological responses prompted by hormone-receptor binding. Lefkowitz also discovered a molecule known as beta-adrenergic receptor kinase (beta-ARK), which regulates GPCR activity.

In 1984 Kobilka joined Lefkowitz's research group at Duke. Lefkowitz was then trying to determine the DNA sequence of the beta2-adrenergic receptor. Kobilka proceeded to piece together the DNA sequence using bacteria that had been genetically engineered to produce large quantities of genomic DNA, thereby overcoming the limitations imposed by the receptor's restricted natural production in cells. Kobilka's breakthrough facilitated the team's discovery that all GPCRs possess seven domains that cross through the cell membrane; those domains were found to be fundamental to the receptors' activity. Lefkowitz later identified a protein called beta-arrestin, which acts on beta-ARK-phosphorylated GPCRs and which explained the

(Continued on the next page)

(Continued from the previous page)

phenomenon of GPCR desensitization in response to repeated agonist binding.

In 1989–90 Kobilka established a laboratory at Stanford University, where he had received a professorship in medicine and molecular and cellular physiology. He continued to investigate the relationship between GPCR structure and function, using adrenergic receptors as model systems. He became known for his application of innovative biophysical techniques, most notably his use of X-ray crystallography, in which an X-ray beam is projected onto a protein crystal to create a diffraction pattern that can then be used to deduce the protein's atomic structure in three dimensions. Kobilka spent two decades working out a process to generate protein crystals of the beta2-adrenergic receptor that were sufficiently large for synchrotron analysis. The receptor's shifting conformation further complicated the crystallization process. In 2011, however, having enlisted the help of colleagues in the United States and Europe, Kobilka finally published the first high-resolution view of transmembrane signaling by the beta2 receptor. The development was considered a milestone in biology and made possible the production of crystals of other GPCRs. Of particular significance was the opportunity to investigate the structures of GPCRs of pharmacological relevance, which could facilitate the development of drugs that targeted specific receptors, thereby enhancing therapeutic benefits while minimizing side effects.

Both inborn and acquired mutations in genes encoding GPCRs can give rise to disease in humans. For example, an inborn mutation of rhodopsin results in continuous activation of intracellular signaling molecules, which causes congenital night blindness. In addition, acquired mutations in certain GPCRs cause abnormal increases in receptor activity and expression in cell membranes, which can give rise to cancer. Because GPCRs play specific roles in human disease, they have provided useful targets for drug development. The antipsychotic agents clozapine and olanzapine block specific GPCRs that normally bind dopamine or serotonin. By blocking the receptors, these drugs disrupt the neural pathways that give rise to symptoms of schizophrenia. There also exist a variety of agents that stimulate GPCR activity. The drugs salmeterol and albuterol, which bind to and activate beta-adrenergic GPCRs, stimulate airway opening in the lungs and thus are used in the treatment of some respiratory conditions, including chronic obstructive pulmonary disease and asthma.

SECOND MESSENGERS

Second messengers are molecules found inside cells that act to transmit signals from receptors to targets. The term *second messenger* was coined upon the discovery of these substances in order to distinguish them from hormones and other molecules that function outside the cell as "first messengers" in the transmission of biological information. Many second messenger molecules are small and therefore diffuse rapidly through the cytoplasm, enabling information to move quickly throughout the cell. As elements of signaling pathways, second messengers can serve to integrate information when multiple independent upstream inputs influence the rates of synthesis and degradation of the second messenger. In addition, second messengers can have multiple downstream targets, thereby expanding the scope of signal transmission.

A large number of second messenger molecules have been characterized, including cyclic nucleotides (e.g., cyclic adenosine monophosphate, or cAMP, and cyclic guanosine monophosphate, or cGMP), ions (e.g., Ca^{2+}), phospholipid-derived molecules (e.g., inositol triphosphate), and even a gas, nitric oxide (NO). The calcium ion Ca^{2+} has a critical role in the rapid responses of neurons and muscle cells. At rest, cells maintain a low concentration of Ca^{2+} in the cytoplasm, expending energy to pump these ions out of the cell. When activated, neurons and muscle cells rapidly increase their cytoplasmic Ca^{2+} concentration by opening channels in the cell membrane, which allow Ca^{2+} ions outside the cell to enter rapidly.

The cyclic nucleotide cAMP is synthesized by adenylyl cyclase enzymes, which are downstream of heterotrimeric G-proteins (guanine nucleotide binding proteins) and receptors. For example, when epinephrine binds to beta-adrenergic receptors in cell membranes, G-protein activation stimulates cAMP synthesis by adenylyl cyclase. The newly synthesized cAMP is then able to act as a second messenger, rapidly propagating the epinephrine signal to the appropriate molecules in the cell. This stimulatory signaling pathway leads to the production of effects such as increasing rate and force of contraction of the heart that are characteristic of epinephrine. Caffeine also enhances the action of cAMP by inhibiting the enzyme phosphodiesterase, which degrades cAMP. The enhancement of cAMP activity contributes to the general stimulatory action of caffeine. As a gas, nitric oxide (NO) is distinct among second messengers in being able to diffuse across cell membranes, which allows signal information to cross into neighbouring cells.

ION CHANNELS

An ion channel is a protein expressed by cells that creates a pathway for charged ions from dissolved salts, including sodium, potassium, calcium, and chloride ions, to pass through the otherwise impermeant lipid cell membrane. Operation of cells in the nervous system, contraction of the heart and of skeletal muscle, and secretion in the pancreas are

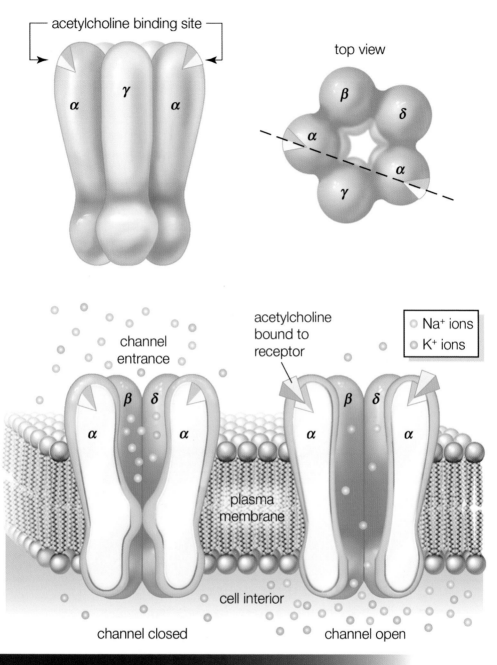

The nicotinic acetylcholine receptor is an example of a ligand-gated ion channel. It is composed of five subunits arranged symmetrically around a central conducting pore. Upon binding acetylcholine, the channel opens and allows diffusion of sodium (Na⁺) and potassium (K⁺) ions through the conducting pore.

examples of physiological processes that require ion channels. In addition, ion channels in the membranes of intracellular organelles are important for regulating cytoplasmic calcium concentration and acidification of specific subcellular compartments (e.g., lysosomes).

Ions flow passively through channels toward equilibrium. This movement may be driven by electrical (voltage) or chemical (concentration) gradients. The ability to alter ion flow as a result of the development of ion channels may have provided an evolutionary advantage by allowing single-celled organisms to regulate their volume in the face of environmental changes. Through subsequent evolution, ion channels have come to play essential roles in cellular secretion and electrical signaling.

Most ion channels are gated—that is, they open and close either spontaneously or in response to a specific stimulus, such as the binding of a small molecule to the channel protein (ligand-gated ion channels) or a change in voltage across the membrane that is sensed by charged segments of the channel protein (voltage-gated ion channels). In addition, most ion channels are selective, allowing only certain ions to pass through. Some channels conduct only one type of ion (e.g., potassium), whereas other channels exhibit relative selectivity—for example, allowing positively charged cations to pass through while excluding negatively charged anions. Cells in higher organisms may express more than 100 different types of ion channel, each with different selectivity and different gating properties.

The flow of charged ions through open channels represents an electrical current that changes the voltage across the membrane by altering the distribution of charge. In excitable cells, voltage-gated channels that allow transient influx of positive ions (e.g., sodium and calcium ions) underlie brief depolarizations of the membrane known as action potentials. Action potentials can be transmitted rapidly over long distances, allowing for coordination and precise timing of physiological outputs. In nearly all cases, action potentials trigger downstream physiological effects, such as secretion or muscle contraction, by opening voltage-gated calcium-selective ion channels and elevating intracellular calcium concentration.

The amino acid sequences of many different ion channel proteins have been determined, and in a few cases the X-ray crystal structure of the channel is known as well. Based on their structure, the majority of ion channels can be classified into six or seven superfamilies. For potassium-selective channels, which are among the best-characterized ion channels, four homologous transmembrane subunits come together to create a tunnel, known as the conducting pore, that provides a polar pathway through the nonpolar lipid membrane. Other channel types

DISCOVERING THE PATCH-CLAMP TECHNIQUE

German scientists Bert Sakmann (1942–) and Erwin Neher (1944–) won the 1991 Nobel Prize for Physiology or Medicine for research into basic cell function and for their development of the patch-clamp technique—a laboratory method widely used in cell biology and neuroscience to detect electrical currents as small as a trillionth of an ampere through cell membranes.

From 1969 to 1970 Sakmann served as a research assistant in the department of neurophysiology at the Max Planck Institute for Psychiatry and then finished his postdoctoral studies in the department of biophysics at University College, London. After receiving his medical degree from the University of Göttingen in 1974, Sakmann joined the department of neurobiology at the Max Planck Institute for Biophysical Chemistry, where he shared laboratory space with Neher. Neher first developed the idea of the patch-clamp technique in his doctoral thesis.

The two men used the patch-clamp technique to conclusively establish the existence of characteristic sets of ion channels in cell membranes—some of which permit the flow of only positive ions, while others pass only negatively charged ions. This established, they examined a broad range of cellular functions, eventually discovering the role that ion

(Continued on the next page)

(Continued from the previous page)

channels play in such diseases as diabetes, cystic fibrosis, epilepsy, several cardiovascular diseases, and certain neuromuscular disorders. These discoveries enabled the development of new and more specific drug therapies.

Ongoing basic research on ion channels seeks to understand the structural basis for permeability, ion selectivity, and gating at the molecular level. Research efforts also attempt to answer questions about the cellular regulation of ion channel protein synthesis and about the subcellular distribution and ultimate degradation of channels. In addition, compounds with greater specificity and potency for channels involved in pain sensation, cardiovascular disease, and other pathological conditions are potential sources for drug development.

require either three or five homologous subunits to generate the central conducting pore. In solution, ions are stabilized by polarized water molecules in the surrounding environment. Narrow, highly selective ion channels mimic the water environment by lining the conducting pore with polarized carbonyl oxygen atoms. Less selective channels form pores with a diameter large enough that ions and water molecules may pass through together.

Many natural toxins target ion channels. Examples include the voltage-gated sodium channel blocker tetrodotoxin, which is produced by bacteria resident in puffers (blowfish) and several other organisms; the irreversible nicotinic acetylcholine receptor antagonist alpha-bungarotoxin, from the venom of snakes in the genus *Bungarus* (kraits); and plant-derived alkaloids, such as strychnine and d-tubocurarine, which inhibit the activation of ion channels that are opened by the neurotransmitters glycine and acetylcholine, respectively. In addition, a large number of therapeutic drugs, including local anesthetics, benzodiazepines, and sulfonylurea derivatives, act directly or indirectly to modulate ion channel activity.

Inherited mutations in ion channel genes and in genes encoding proteins that regulate ion channel activity have been implicated in a number of diseases, including ataxia (the inability to coordinate voluntary muscle movements), diabetes mellitus, certain types of epilepsy, and cardiac arrhythmias (irregularities in heartbeat). For example, genetic variations in sodium-selective and potassium-selective channels, or in their associated regulatory subunits, underlie some forms of long-QT syndrome. This syndrome is characterized by a prolongation in the depolarization time-course of cardiac myocyte action potentials, which can lead to fatal arrhythmias. In addition, mutations in ATP-sensitive potassium channels that control insulin secretion from cells in the pancreas underlie some forms of diabetes mellitus.

TRANSIENT RECEPTOR POTENTIAL CHANNELS

Transient receptor potential channels (or TRP channels) form a superfamily of ion channels that are involved in various types of sensory reception, including thermoreception, chemoreception, mechanoreception, and photoreception. TRP channels were discovered in the late 1970s and early 1980s on photoreceptors in fruit flies (*Drosophila*). Since then, a number of TRP channels have been identified in a variety of organisms, from nematodes to humans, and have been grouped based on similarities in gene sequence and protein structure. These channels are found in the outer membranes of different types of sensory cells, and their responses to various stimuli are manifested through their functions as ion channels, regulating the flow of ions, such as potassium, calcium, and sodium, into or out of cells. Ion flux can lead to cell membrane depolarization (less negative charge across the cell), which leads to an action potential—a brief electric polarization that results in a nerve impulse and physiological sensation or perception.

The major groups of TRP channels include TRPM (melastatin), TRPV (vanilloid), TRPC (canonical), TRPP (polycystin), TRPML (mucolipin), and TRPA (subfamily A). TRPM, TRPA, and TRPV channels can respond to changes in temperature, with TRPM and TRPA known to respond to cold and TRPV known to respond to warmth, noxious heat, and pain. TRPV channels have been identified on sensory neurons and on epithelial cells, and TRPM channels are primarily expressed on C-fibres in peripheral nerves. TRPC channels are expressed primarily on smooth muscle and heart cells and appear to regulate certain responses in the central nervous system and in the vasculature. TRPP channels are expressed on kidney cells and on the cells of the retina and may play a role in controlling the responses of cilia to fluid flow in the renal epithelium. In mice certain TRPC channels are pheromone-sensitive, and in humans some TRPM channels are capable of distinguishing among tastes, including sweet, bitter, and umami (meaty).

INTERCELLULAR COMMUNICATION BETWEEN PLANT CELLS

Similar to the gap junction of animal cells is the plasmodesma, a channel passing through the cell wall and allowing direct molecular communication between adjacent plant cells. Plasmodesmata are lined with cell membrane, in effect uniting all connected cells with one continuous cell membrane. Running down the middle of each channel is a thin membranous tube that connects the endoplasmic reticula (ER) of the two cells. This structure is a remnant of the ER of the original parent cell, which, as the parent cell divided, was caught in the developing cell plate. Although the precise mechanisms are not fully understood, the plasmodesma is thought to regulate the passage of small molecules such as salts, sugars, and amino acids by constricting or dilating the openings at each end of the channel.

The discovery of cell wall fragments with regulatory functions opened a new era in plant research. For years scientists had been puzzled by the chemical complexity of cell wall polysaccharides, which far exceeds the structural requirements of plant cell walls. The answer came when it was found that specific fragments of cell wall polysaccharides, called oligosaccharins, are able to induce specific responses in plant cells and tissues. One such fragment, released by enzymes used by fungi to break down plant cell walls, consists of a linear polymer of 10 to 12 galacturonic acid residues. Exposure of plant cells to such fragments induces them to produce antibiotics known as phytoalexins. In other experiments it has been shown that exposing strips of tobacco stem cells to a different type of cell wall fragment leads to the growth of roots. Other fragments lead to the formation of stems, and yet others to the production of flowers. In all instances the concentration of oligosaccharins required to bring about the observed responses is equal to that of hormones in animal cells. Indeed, oligosaccharins may be viewed as the oligosaccharide hormones of plants.

CELL DIVISION AND DIFFERENTIATION

I n unicellular organisms, cell division is the means of reproduction. In multicellular organisms, it is the means of tissue growth and maintenance. Survival of multicellular eukaryotes depends upon interactions between many cell types, and it is essential that a balanced distribution of types be maintained. This is achieved by the highly regulated process of cell proliferation. The growth and division of different cell populations are regulated in different ways, but the basic mechanisms are similar throughout multicellular organisms.

Most tissues of the body grow by increasing their cell number, but this growth is highly regulated to maintain a balance between different tissues. In adults most cell division is involved in tissue renewal rather than growth, with many types of cells undergoing continuous replacement. Skin cells, for example, are constantly being sloughed off and replaced. In this case, the mature differentiated cells do not divide, but their population is renewed by division of immature stem cells. In certain other cells, such as those of the liver, mature cells remain capable of division to allow growth or regeneration after injury.

In contrast to these patterns, other types of cells either cannot divide or are prevented from dividing by certain molecules produced by nearby cells. As a result, in the adult organism, some tissues have a greatly reduced capacity to renew damaged or diseased cells. Examples of such tissues include heart muscle, nerve cells of the central nervous system, and lens cells in mammals. Maintenance and repair of these cells is limited to replacing intracellular components rather than replacing entire cells.

DUPLICATION OF GENETIC INFORMATION

Before a cell can divide, it must accurately and completely duplicate the genetic information encoded in its DNA in order for its progeny cells to function and survive. This is a complex problem because of the great length of DNA molecules. Each human chromosome consists of a long double spiral, or helix, each strand of which consists of more than 100 million nucleotides.

The duplication of DNA is called DNA replication, and it is initiated by complex enzymes called DNA polymerases. These progress along the molecule, reading the sequences of nucleotides that are linked together to make DNA chains. Each strand of the DNA double helix, therefore, acts as a template specifying the nucleotide structure of a new growing chain. After replication, each of the two daughter DNA double helices consists of one parental DNA strand wound around one newly synthesized DNA strand.

In order for DNA to replicate, the two strands must be unwound from each other. Enzymes called helicases unwind the two DNA strands, and additional proteins bind to the separated strands to stabilize them and prevent them from pairing again. In addition, a remarkable class of enzyme called DNA topoisomerase removes the helical twists by cutting either one or both strands and then resealing the cut. These enzymes can also untangle and unknot DNA when it is tightly coiled into a chromatin fibre.

In the circular DNA of prokaryotes, replication starts at a unique site called the origin of replication and then proceeds in both directions around the molecule until the two processes meet, producing two daughter molecules.

In rapidly growing prokaryotes, a second round of replication can start before the first has finished. The situation in eukaryotes is more complicated, as replication moves more slowly than in prokaryotes. At 500 to 5,000 nucleotides per minute (versus 100,000 nucleotides per minute in prokaryotes), it would take a human chromosome about a month to replicate if started at a single site. Actually, replication begins at many sites on the long chromosomes of animals, plants, and fungi. Distances between adjacent initiation sites are not always the same—for example, they are closer in the rapidly dividing embryonic cells of frogs or flies than in adult cells of the same species.

Accurate DNA replication is crucial to ensure that daughter cells have exact copies of the genetic information for synthesizing proteins. Accuracy is achieved by a "proofreading" ability of the DNA polymerase itself. It can erase its own errors and then synthesize anew. There are also repair systems that correct genetic damage to DNA. For example, the incorporation of an incorrect nucleotide, or damage caused by mutagenic agents, can be corrected by cutting out a section of the daughter strand and recopying the parental strand.

CELL DIVISION

In eukaryotes, cell division may occur by one of two major processes: mitosis or meiosis. Mitosis is a process of cell duplication, or reproduction, during which one cell gives rise to two genetically identical daughter cells. Mitosis is performed by somatic, or body, cells such as skin cells and muscle cells. In contrast, meiosis is a form of cell division that is carried out only by germ cells, which give rise to the reproductive cells (e.g., sperm and eggs). Meiosis is much more elaborate than mitosis, since it involves two fissions of the nucleus. These fissions give rise to four mature gametes, or sex cells, each possessing half the number of chromosomes of the original cell. Each gamete is capable of combining with a sexually compatible gamete (e.g., sperm-egg fusion) to generate a new organism.

MITOSIS AND CYTOKINESIS

In eukaryotes the processes of DNA replication and cell division occur at different times of the cell division cycle. During cell division, DNA condenses to form short, tightly coiled, rodlike chromosomes. Each chromosome then splits longitudinally, forming two identical chromatids. Each pair of chromatids is divided between the two daughter cells during mitosis, or division of the nucleus, a process in which the chromosomes are propelled by attachment to a bundle of microtubules called the mitotic spindle.

Mitosis can be divided into five phases. In prophase the mitotic spindle forms and the chromosomes condense. In prometaphase the nuclear envelope breaks down (in many but not all eukaryotes) and the chromosomes attach to the mitotic spindle.

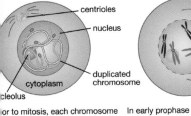

centrioles

nucleus

duplicated chromosome

cytoplasm

nucleolus

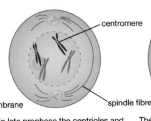

aster

centromere

nuclear membrane

spindle fibre

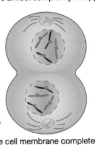

Prior to mitosis, each chromosome makes an exact duplicate of itself. The chromosomes then thicken and coil.

In early prophase the centrioles, which have divided, form asters and move apart. The nuclear membrane begins to disintegrate.

In late prophase the centrioles and asters are at opposite poles. The nucleolus and nuclear membrane have almost completely disappeared.

The doubled chromosomes—their centromeres attached to the spindle fibres—line up at mid-cell in metaphase.

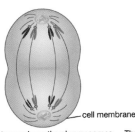

cell membrane

In early anaphase the centromeres split. Half the chromosomes move to one pole, half to the other pole.

In late anaphase the chromosomes have almost reached their respective poles. The cell membrane begins to pinch at the centre.

The cell membrane completes constriction in telophase. Nuclear membranes form around the separated chromosomes.

At mitosis completion, there are two cells with the same structures and number of chromosomes as the parent cell.

One cell gives rise to two genetically identical daughter cells during the process of mitosis.

Both chromatids of each chromosome attach to the spindle at a specialized chromosomal region called the kinetochore. In metaphase the condensed chromosomes align in a plane across the equator of the mitotic spindle. Anaphase follows as the separated chromatids move abruptly toward opposite spindle poles. Finally, in telophase a new nuclear envelope forms around each set of unraveling chromatids.

An essential feature of mitosis is the attachment of the chromatids to opposite poles of the mitotic spindle. This ensures that each of the daughter cells will receive a complete set of chromosomes. The mitotic spindle is composed of microtubules, each of which is a tubular assembly of molecules of the protein tubulin. Some microtubules extend from one spindle pole to the other, while a second class extends from one spindle pole to a chromatid. Microtubules can grow or shrink by the addition or removal of tubulin molecules. The shortening of spindle microtubules at anaphase propels attached chromatids to the spindle poles, where they unravel to form new nuclei. The two poles of the mitotic spindle are occupied by centrosomes, which organize the microtubule arrays. In animal cells each centrosome contains a pair of cylindrical centrioles, which are themselves composed of complex arrays of microtubules. Centrioles duplicate at a precise time in the cell division cycle, usually close to the start of DNA replication.

After mitosis comes cytokinesis, the division of the cytoplasm. This is another process in which animal and plant cells differ. In animal cells cytokinesis is achieved through the constriction of the cell by a ring of contractile microfilaments consisting of actin and myosin, the proteins involved in muscle contraction and other forms of cell movement. In plant cells the cytoplasm is divided by the formation of a new cell wall, called the cell plate, between the two daughter cells. The cell plate arises from small Golgi-derived vesicles that coalesce in a plane across the equator of the late telophase spindle to form a disk-shaped structure. In this process, each vesicle contributes

DISCOVERING MITOSIS

German scientists Eduard Adolf Strasburger (1844–1912) and Walther Flemming (1843–1905) were the first to identify and explain the process of mitosis. Strausburger set forth the basic principles of mitosis in his *Über Zellbildung und Zelltheilung* (1876; "On Cell Formation and Cell Division"), and in each succeeding edition he clarified and modified the description of the process until in the third edition (1880) he enunciated one of the modern laws of plant cytology: New nuclei can arise only from the division of other nuclei.

A pioneer in the use of newly discovered aniline dyes to visualize cell structures, Flemming found (1879) that a certain class of dyes revealed a thread-like material in the nucleus. Applying these stains to cells killed at different stages of division, he prepared a series of slides that, upon microscopic examination, clearly established the sequence of changes occurring in the nucleus during cell division. He showed that the threads (later called chromosomes) shortened and seemed to split longitudinally into two halves, each half moving to opposite sides of the cell. He named the entire process mitosis and described it in his historic book *Zell-substanz, Kern und Zelltheilung* (1882; "Cell-Substance, Nucleus, and Cell-Division"). The implications of Flemming's work for heredity were not fully appreciated until the recognition of Gregor Mendel's principles of heredity 20 years later.

(Continued on the next page)

(Continued from the previous page)

In 1882 Strasburger devised the terms *cytoplasm* and *nucleoplasm* to describe the cell body and nucleus, respectively. Next, he showed that during fertilization in the flowering plants the nucleus is the primary structure concerned in heredity. In 1888 he established that the nuclei of the germ cells of angiosperms undergo meiosis—a reduction division yielding nuclei with half the number of chromosomes of the original nuclei.

its membrane to the forming cell membranes and its matrix contents to the forming cell wall. A second set of vesicles extends the edge of the cell plate until it reaches and fuses with the sides of the parent cell, thereby completely separating the two new daughter cells. At this point, cellulose synthesis commences, and the cell plate becomes a primary cell wall.

MEIOSIS

A specialized division of chromosomes called meiosis occurs during the formation of the reproductive cells, or gametes, of sexually reproducing organisms. Gametes such as ova, sperm, and pollen begin as germ cells, which, like other types of cells, have two copies of each gene in their nuclei. The chromosomes composed of these matching genes are called homologs. During DNA replication, each chromosome duplicates into two attached chromatids. The homologous chromosomes are then separated to opposite poles of the meiotic spindle by microtubules similar to those of the mitotic spindle. At this stage in the meiosis of germ cells, there is a crucial difference from the mitosis of other cells. In meiosis the two chromatids making up each chromosome remain together, so that whole chromosomes are separated from their homologous partners. Cell

Meiosis, or sex cell division

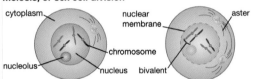

cytoplasm   nuclear membrane   aster   crossing over   centrioles

chromosome

nucleolus   nucleus   bivalent   tetrad   spindle fiber

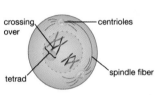

At the onset of meiosis, DNA strands thicken into chromosomes. Homologous, or like, chromosomes begin to approach each other.

Homologous chromosomes pair to form bivalents. The centrioles divide and move to opposite poles of the cell.

The bivalents duplicate to form tetrads, or four-chromatid groups. The nuclear membrane disintegrates. Crossing over (recombination) occurs.

In metaphase I, the tetrads, attached to spindle fibers at their centromeres, line up at mid-cell.

cell membrane

In early anaphase I, the tetrads separate, and the paired chromatids move along the spindle to their respective centrioles.

In late anaphase I, the chromatids have almost reached the spindle poles. The cell membrane begins to constrict.

In telophase I, nuclear membranes enclose the separated chromatids. The cell membrane completes its constriction.

The first meiotic division ends. There are now two cells, each with the same number of chromatids as the parent cell.

Prophase II begins. In the second meiotic division, homologous chromatids do not duplicate but merely separate.

In metaphase II, the chromatids line up at mid-cell. The centrioles and asters are at the poles. A spindle has formed.

In anaphase II, the now-separated chromatids approach their respective poles. The cell membrane begins to constrict.

Telophase II has been completed There are now four cells, each with half the number of chromosomes of the parent cell.

The formation of gametes (sex cells) occurs during the process of meiosis.

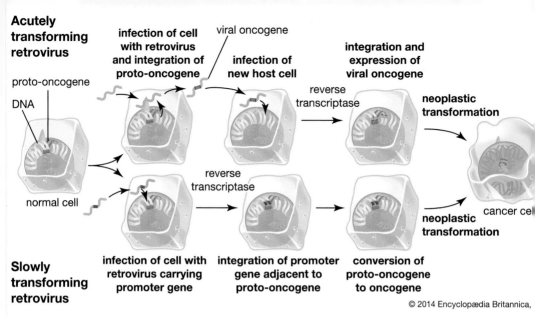

Retroviral insertion can convert a proto-oncogene, integral to the control of cell division, into an oncogene, the agent responsible for transforming a healthy cell into a cancer cell. An acutely transforming retrovirus (*shown at top*), which produces tumours within weeks of infection, incorporates genetic material from a host cell into its own genome upon infection, forming a viral oncogene. When the viral oncogene infects another cell, an enzyme called reverse transcriptase copies the single-stranded genetic material into double-stranded DNA, which is then integrated into the cellular genome. A slowly transforming retrovirus (*shown at bottom*), which requires months to elicit tumour growth, does not disrupt cellular function through the insertion of a viral oncogene. Rather, it carries a promoter gene that is integrated into the cellular genome of the host cell next to or within a proto-oncogene, allowing conversion of the proto-oncogene to an oncogene.

tids. The homologous chromosomes are then separated to opposite poles of the meiotic spindle by microtubules similar to those of the mitotic spindle. At this stage in the meiosis of germ cells, there is a crucial difference from the mitosis of other cells. In meiosis the two chromatids making up each chromosome remain together, so that whole chromosomes are separated from their homologous partners. Cell

Meiosis, or sex cell division

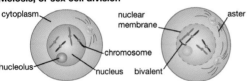
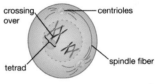

cytoplasm — nuclear membrane — aster — crossing over — centrioles

nucleolus — chromosome — nucleus — bivalent — tetrad — spindle fiber

At the onset of meiosis, DNA strands thicken into chromosomes. Homologous, or like, chromosomes begin to approach each other.

Homologous chromosomes pair to form bivalents. The centrioles divide and move to opposite poles of the cell.

The bivalents duplicate to form tetrads, or four-chromatid groups. The nuclear membrane disintegrates. Crossing over (recombination) occurs.

In metaphase I, the tetrads, attached to spindle fibers at their centromeres, line up at mid-cell.

cell membrane

In early anaphase I, the tetrads separate, and the paired chromatids move along the spindle to their respective centrioles.

In late anaphase I, the chromatids have almost reached the spindle poles. The cell membrane begins to constrict.

In telophase I, nuclear membranes enclose the separated chromatids. The cell membrane completes its constriction.

The first meiotic division ends. There are now two cells, each with the same number of chromatids as the parent cell.

Prophase II begins. In the second meiotic division, homologous chromatids do not duplicate but merely separate.

In metaphase II, the chromatids line up at mid-cell. The centrioles and asters are at the poles. A spindle has formed.

In anaphase II, the now-separated chromatids approach their respective poles. The cell membrane begins to constrict.

Telophase II has been completed. There are now four cells, each with half the number of chromosomes of the parent cell.

The formation of gametes (sex cells) occurs during the process of meiosis.

division then occurs, followed by a second division that resembles mitosis more closely in that it separates the two chromatids of each remaining chromosome. In this way, when meiosis is complete, each mature gamete receives only one copy of each gene instead of the two copies present in other cells.

CELL DIVISION CYCLE

In prokaryotes, DNA synthesis can take place uninterrupted between cell divisions, and new cycles of DNA synthesis can begin before previous cycles have finished. In contrast, eukaryotes duplicate their DNA exactly once during a discrete period between cell divisions. This period is called the S (for synthetic) phase. It is preceded by a period called G_1 (meaning "first gap") and followed by a period called G_2, during which nuclear DNA synthesis does not occur.

The four periods G_1, S, G_2, and M (for mitosis) make up the cell division cycle. The cell cycle characteristically lasts between 10 and 20 hours in rapidly proliferating adult cells, but it can be arrested for weeks or months in quiescent cells or for a lifetime in neurons of the brain. Prolonged arrest of this type usually occurs during the G_1 phase and is sometimes referred to as G_0. In contrast, some embryonic cells, such as those of fruit flies (vinegar flies), can complete entire cycles and divide in only 11 minutes. In these exceptional cases, G_1 and G_2 are undetectable, and mitosis alternates with DNA synthesis. In addition, the duration of the S phase varies dramatically. The fruit fly embryo takes only four minutes to replicate its DNA, compared with several hours in adult cells of the same species.

CONTROLLED PROLIFERATION

Several studies have identified the transition from the G_1 to the S phase as a crucial control point of the cell cycle. Stimuli are known to cause resting cells to proliferate by inducing them to leave G_1 and begin DNA synthesis. These stimuli, called growth factors, are naturally occurring proteins specific to certain groups of cells in the body.

They include nerve growth factor, epidermal growth factor, and platelet-derived growth factor. Such factors may have important roles in the healing of wounds as well as in the maintenance and growth of normal tissues. Many growth factors are known to act on the external membrane of the cell, by interacting with specialized protein receptor molecules. These respond by triggering further cellular changes, including an increase in calcium levels that makes the cell interior more alkaline and the addition of phosphate groups to the amino acid tyrosine in proteins. The complex response of cells to growth factors is of fundamental importance to the control of cell proliferation.

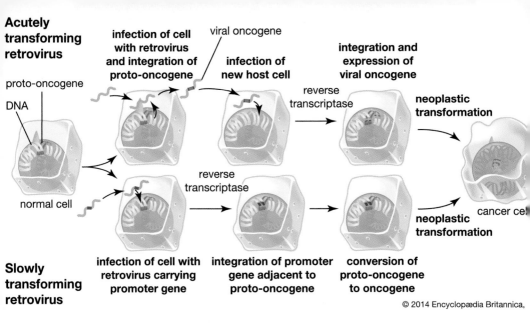

Acutely transforming retrovirus

infection of cell with retrovirus and integration of proto-oncogene

viral oncogene

infection of new host cell

integration and expression of viral oncogene

proto-oncogene

DNA

reverse transcriptase

neoplastic transformation

normal cell

reverse transcriptase

cancer cell

neoplastic transformation

Slowly transforming retrovirus

infection of cell with retrovirus carrying promoter gene

integration of promoter gene adjacent to proto-oncogene

conversion of proto-oncogene to oncogene

© 2014 Encyclopædia Britannica,

Retroviral insertion can convert a proto-oncogene, integral to the control of cell division, into an oncogene, the agent responsible for transforming a healthy cell into a cancer cell. An acutely transforming retrovirus (*shown at top*), which produces tumours within weeks of infection, incorporates genetic material from a host cell into its own genome upon infection, forming a viral oncogene. When the viral oncogene infects another cell, an enzyme called reverse transcriptase copies the single-stranded genetic material into double-stranded DNA, which is then integrated into the cellular genome. A slowly transforming retrovirus (*shown at bottom*), which requires months to elicit tumour growth, does not disrupt cellular function through the insertion of a viral oncogene. Rather, it carries a promoter gene that is integrated into the cellular genome of the host cell next to or within a proto-oncogene, allowing conversion of the proto-oncogene to an oncogene.

FAILURE OF PROLIFERATION CONTROL

Cancer can arise when the controlling factors over cell growth fail and allow a cell and its descendants to keep dividing at the expense of the organism. Studies of viruses that transform cultured cells and thus lead to the loss of control of cell growth have provided insight into the mechanisms that drive the formation of tumours. Transformed cells may differ from their normal progenitors by continuing to proliferate at very high densities, in the absence of growth factors, or in the absence of a solid substrate for support.

Major advances in the understanding of growth control have come from studies of the viral genes that cause transformation. These viral oncogenes have led to the identification of related cellular genes called protooncogenes. Protooncogenes can be altered by mutation or epigenetic modification, which converts them into oncogenes and leads to cell transformation. Specific oncogenes are activated in particular human cancers. For example, an oncogene called RAS is associated with many epithelial cancers, while another, called MYC, is associated with leukemias.

An interesting feature of oncogenes is that they may act at different levels corresponding to the multiple steps seen in the development of cancer. Some oncogenes immortalize cells so that they divide indefinitely, whereas normal cells die after a limited number of generations. Other oncogenes transform cells so that they grow in the absence of growth factors. A combination of these two functions leads to loss of proliferation control, whereas each of these functions on its own cannot. The mode of action of oncogenes also provides important clues to the nature of growth control and cancer. For example, some oncogenes are known to encode receptors for growth factors that may cause continuous proliferation in the absence of appropriate growth factors.

Loss of growth control has the added consequence that cells no longer repair their DNA effectively, and thus aberrant mitoses occur. As a result, additional mutations arise that subvert a cell's normal constraints to remain in its tissue of origin. Epithelial tumour cells, for example, acquire the ability to cross the basal lamina and enter the bloodstream or lymphatic system, where they migrate to other parts of the body, a process called metastasis. When cells metastasize to distant tissues, the tumour is described as malignant, whereas prior to metastasis a tumour is described as benign.

CELL DIFFERENTIATION

Adult organisms are composed of a number of distinct cell types. Cells are organized into tissues, each of which typically contains a small number of

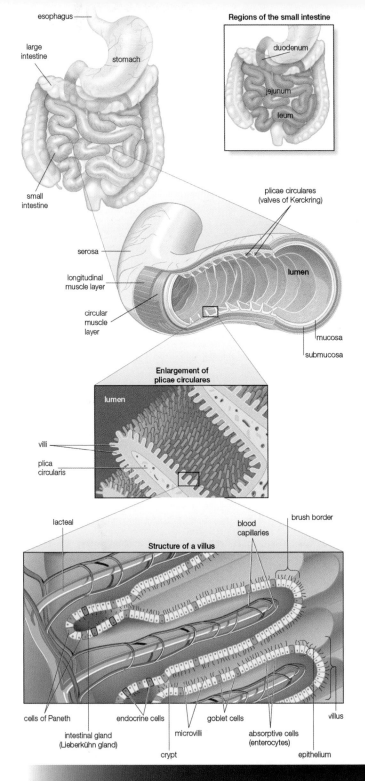

Regions of the small intestine

esophagus

large intestine

stomach

duodenum

jejunum

ileum

small intestine

plicae circulares (valves of Kerckring)

serosa

lumen

longitudinal muscle layer

circular muscle layer

mucosa

submucosa

Enlargement of plicae circulares

lumen

villi

plica circularis

lacteal

blood capillaries

brush border

Structure of a villus

cells of Paneth

endocrine cells

goblet cells

villus

intestinal gland (Lieberkühn gland)

microvilli

absorptive cells (enterocytes)

crypt

epithelium

The small intestine contains many distinct types of cells, each of which serves a specific function.

cell types and is devoted to a specific physiological function. For example, the epithelial tissue lining the small intestine contains columnar absorptive cells, mucus-secreting goblet cells, hormone-secreting endocrine cells, and enzyme-secreting Paneth cells. In addition, there exist undifferentiated dividing cells that lie in the crypts between the intestinal villi and serve to replace the other cell types when they become damaged or worn out. Another example of a differentiated tissue is the skeletal tissue of a long bone, which contains osteoblasts (large cells that synthesize bone) in the outer sheath and osteocytes (mature bone cells) and osteoclasts (multinucleate cells involved in bone remodeling) within the matrix.

In general, the simpler the overall organization of the animal, the fewer the number of distinct cell types that they possess. Mammals contain more than 200 different cell types, whereas simple invertebrate animals may have only a few different types. Plants are also made up of differentiated cells, but they are quite different from the cells of animals. For example, a leaf in a higher plant is covered with a cuticle layer of epidermal cells. Among these are pores composed of two specialized cells, which regulate gaseous exchange across the epidermis. Within the leaf is the mesophyll, a spongy tissue responsible for photosynthetic activity. There are also veins composed of xylem elements, which transport water up

from the soil, and phloem elements, which transport products of photosynthesis to the storage organs.

The various cell types have traditionally been recognized and classified according to their appearance in the light microscope following the process offixing, processing, sectioning, and staining tissues that is known as histology. Classical histology has been augmented by a variety of more discriminating techniques. Electron microscopy allows for higher magnifications. Histochemistry involves the use of coloured precipitating substrates to stain particular enzymes in situ. Immunohistochemistry uses specific antibodies to identify particular substances, usually proteins or carbohydrates, within cells. In situ hybridization involves the use of nucleic acid probes to visualize the location of specific messenger RNAs (mRNA). These modern methods have allowed the identification of more cell types than could be visualized by classical histology, particularly in the brain, the immune system, and among the hormone-secreting cells of the endocrine system.

STATES OF DIFFERENTIATION

The biochemical basis of cell differentiation is the synthesis by the cell of a particular set of proteins, carbohydrates, and lipids. This synthesis is catalyzed by proteins called enzymes. Each enzyme in turn is synthesized in accordance with a particular

gene, or sequence of nucleotides in the DNA of the cell nucleus. A particular state of differentiation, then, corresponds to the set of genes that is expressed and the level to which it is expressed.

It is believed that all of an organism's genes are present in each cell nucleus, no matter what the cell type, and that differences between tissues are not due to the presence or absence of certain genes but are due to the expression of some and the repression of others. In animals the best evidence for retention of the entire set of genes comes from whole animal cloning experiments in which the nucleus of a differentiated cell is substituted for the nucleus of a fertilized egg. In many species this can result in the development of a normal embryo that contains the full range of body parts and cell types. Likewise, in plants it is often possible to grow complete embryos from individual cells in tissue culture. Such experiments show that any nucleus has the genetic information required for the growth of a developing organism, and they strongly suggest that, for most tissues, cell differentiation arises from the regulation of genetic activity rather than the removal or destruction of unwanted genes. The only known exception to this rule comes from the immune system, where segments of DNA in developing white blood cells are slightly rearranged, producing a wide variety of antibody and receptor molecules.

Fully differentiated cells are qualitatively different from one another. States of terminal differentiation are stable and persistent, both in the lifetime of the cell and in successive cell generations (in the case of differentiated types that are capable of continued cell division). The inherent stability of the differentiated state is maintained by various processes, including feedback activation of genes by their own products and repression of inactive genes. Chromatin structure may be important in maintaining states of differentiation, although it is still unclear whether this can be maintained during DNA replication, which involves temporary removal of chromosomal proteins and unwinding of the DNA double helix.

A type of differentiation control that is maintained during DNA replication is the methylation of DNA, which tends to recruit histone deacetylases and hence close up the structure of the chromatin. DNA methylation occurs when a methyl group is attached to the exterior, or sugar-phosphate side, of a cytosine (C) residue. Cytosine methylation occurs only on a C nucleotide when it is connected to a G (guanine) nucleotide on the same strand of DNA. These nucleotide pairings are called CG dinucleotides. One class of DNA methylase enzyme can introduce new methylations when required, whereas another class, called maintenance methylases, methylates CG dinucleotides in the DNA double helix only when the CG of the complementary strand is already methyl-

ated. Each time the methylated DNA is replicated, the old strand has the methyl groups and the new strand does not. The maintenance methylase will then add methyl groups to all the CGs opposite the existing methyl groups to restore a fully methylated double helix. This mechanism guarantees stability of the DNA methylation pattern, and hence the differentiated state, during the processes of DNA replication and cell division.

TRANSCRIPTION FACTORS

At the molecular level there are many ways in which the expression of a gene can be differentially regulated in different cell types. There may be differences in the copying, or transcription, of the gene into RNA; in the processing of the initial RNA transcript into mRNA; in the control of mRNA movement to the cytoplasm; in the translation of mRNA to protein; or in the stability of mRNA. However, the control of transcription has the most influence over gene expression and has received the most detailed analysis.

The DNA in the cell nucleus exists in the form of chromatin, which is made up of DNA bound to histones (simple alkaline proteins) and other nonhistone proteins. Most of the DNA is complexed into repeating structures called nucleosomes, each of which contains eight molecules of histone. Active genes are found in parts of the DNA where the chromatin

has an "open" configuration, in which regulatory proteins are able to gain access to the DNA. The degree to which the chromatin opens depends on chemical modifications of the outer parts of the histone molecules and on the presence or absence of particular nonhistone proteins. Transcriptional control is exerted with the help of regulatory sequences that are found associated with a gene, such as the promoter sequence, a region near the start of the gene, and enhancer sequences, regions that lie elsewhere within the DNA that augment the activity of enzymes involved in the process of transcription. Whether or not transcription occurs depends on the binding of transcription factors to these regulatory sequences.

Transcription factors are proteins that usually possess a DNA-binding region, which recognizes the specific regulatory sequence in the DNA, and an effector region, which activates or inhibits transcription. Transcription factors are vital for the normal development of an organism, as well as for routine cellular functions and response to disease. They often work by recruiting enzymes that add modifications (e.g., acetyl groups or methyl groups) to or remove modifications from the outer parts of the histone molecules. This controls the folding of the chromatin and the accessibility of the DNA to RNA polymerase and other transcription factors. Cell activities influencing the function of transcription factors include nuclear transport (i.e., import or

export) and posttranslational modification such as phosphorylation.

Transcription factors are a very diverse family of proteins and generally function in multi-subunit protein complexes. Thus, in general, it requires several transcription factors working in combination to activate a gene. Basal, or general, transcription factors are necessary for RNA polymerase to function at a site of transcription in eukaryotes. They are considered the most basic set of proteins needed to activate gene transcription, and they include a number of proteins, such as TFIIA (transcription factor II A) and TFIIB (transcription factor II B), among others. Substantial progress has been made in defining the roles played by each of the proteins that compose the basal transcription factor complex.

During development of multicellular organisms, transcription factors are responsible for dictating the fate of individual cells. For example, homeotic genes control the pattern of body formation, and these genes encode transcription factors that direct cells to form various parts of the body. A homeotic protein can activate one gene but repress another, producing effects that are complementary and necessary for the ordered development of an organism. If a mutation occurs in any of the homeotic transcription factors, an organism will not develop correctly. For example, in fruit flies,

mutation of a particular homeotic gene results in altered transcription, leading to the growth of legs on the head instead of antenna. This is known as the antennapedia mutation.

The complexity of the role of transcription factors in regulating gene expression is illustrated by the chicken *delta 1* crystallin gene, which is normally expressed only in the lens of the eye. This gene has a promoter that contains binding sites for two activating transcription factors and an enhancer that contains binding sites for two other activating transcription factors. There is also an additional enhancer site that can bind either an activator (deltaEF3) or a repressor (deltaEF1). Successful transcription requires that all these sites are occupied by the correct transcription factors.

Transcription factors are a common way in which cells respond to extracellular information, such as environmental stimuli and signals from other cells. Transcription factors can have important roles in cancer, if they influence the activity of genes involved in the cell cycle (or cell division cycle). Transcription factors also can be the products of oncogenes or tumour suppressor genes (genes that keep cancer in check). In addition to controlling the genes and transcription of other transcription factors, these protein complexes can also control the genes responsible for their own transcription, leading to complex feedback control mechanisms.

PROCESS OF DIFFERENTIATION

Differentiation from visibly undifferentiated precursor cells occurs during embryonic development, during metamorphosis of larval forms, and following the separation of parts in asexual reproduction. It also takes place in adult organisms during the renewal of tissues and the regeneration of missing parts. Thus, cell differentiation is an essential and ongoing process at all stages of life.

The visible differentiation of cells is only the last of a progressive sequence of states. In each state, the cell becomes increasingly committed toward one type of cell into which it can develop. States of commitment are sometimes described as specification to represent a reversible type of commitment and as determination to represent an irreversible commitment. Although states of specification and determination both represent differential gene activity, the properties of embryonic cells are not necessarily the same as those of fully differentiated cells. In particular, cells in specification states are usually not stable over prolonged periods of time.

Two mechanisms bring about altered commitments in the different regions of the early embryo: cytoplasmic localization and induction. Cytoplasmic localization is evident in the earliest stages of development of the embryo. During this time, the embryo divides without growth, undergoing cleavage divisions that produce separate cells called blasto-meres. Each blastomere inherits a certain region of the original egg cytoplasm, which may contain one or more regulatory substances called cytoplasmic determinants. When the embryo has become a solid mass of blastomeres (called a morula), it generally consists of two or more differently committed cell populations—a result of the blastomeres having incorporated different cytoplasmic determinants. Cytoplasmic determinants may consist of mRNA or protein in a particular state of activation. An exam-ple of the influence of a cytoplasmic determinant is a receptor called Toll, located in the membranes of fruit fly eggs. Activation of Toll ensures that the blas-tomeres will develop into ventral (underside) struc-tures, while blastomeres containing inactive Toll will produce cells that will develop into dorsal (back) structures.

In induction, the second mechanism of commit-ment, a substance secreted by one group of cells alters the development of another group. In early develop-ment, induction is usually instructive, such that the tissue assumes a different state of commitment in the presence of the signal than it would in the absence of the signal. Inductive signals often take the form of concentration gradients of substances that evoke a number of different responses at different concentra-tions. This leads to the formation of a sequence of groups of cells, each in a different state of specification. For example, in *Xenopus* (clawed frog) the early embryo contains a signaling centre called the organizer that secretes inhibitors of bone morphogenetic proteins (BMPs), leading to a ventral-to-dorsal (belly-to-back) gradient of BMP activity. The activity of BMP in the ventral region of the embryo suppresses the expression of transcription factors involved in the formation of the central nervous system and segmented muscles. Suppression ensures that these structures are formed only on the dorsal side, where there is decreased activity of BMP.

The final stage of differentiation often involves the formation of several types of differentiated cells from one precursor or stem cell population. Terminal differentiation occurs not only in embryonic development but also in many tissues in postnatal life. Control of this process depends on a system of lateral inhibition in which cells that are differentiating along a particular pathway send out signals that repress similar differentiation by their neighbours. For example, in the developing central nervous system of vertebrates, neurons arise from a simple tube of neuroepithelium, the cells of which possess a surface receptor called Notch. These cells also possess another cell surface molecule called Delta that can bind to and activate Notch on adjacent cells. Activation of Notch initiates a cascade of intracellular events that results in suppression of Delta production and suppression of neuronal differentiation.

This means that the neuroepithelium generates only a few cells with high expression of Delta surrounded by a larger number of cells with low expression of Delta. High Delta production and low Notch activation makes the cells develop into neurons. Low Delta production and high Notch activation makes the cells remain as precursor cells or become glial (supporting) cells. A similar mechanism is known to produce the endocrine cells of the pancreas and the goblet cells of the intestinal epithelium. Such lateral inhibition systems work because cells in a population are never quite identical to begin with. There are always small differences, such as in the number of Delta molecules displayed on the cell surface. The mechanism of lateral inhibition amplifies these small differences, using them to bring about differential gene expression that leads to stable and persistent states of cell differentiation.

ERRORS

Three classes of abnormal cell differentiation are dysplasia, metaplasia, and anaplasia. Dysplasia indicates an abnormal arrangement of cells, usually arising from a disturbance in their normal growth behaviour. Some dysplasias are precursor lesions to cancer, whereas others are harmless and regress spontaneously. For example, dysplasia of the uterine cervix, called cervical intraepithelial neoplasia (CIN), may progress to cervical cancer. It can be detected by cervical smear cytology tests (Pap smears).

Metaplasia is the conversion of one cell type into another. In fact, it is not usually the differentiated cells themselves that change but rather the stem cell population from which they are derived. Metaplasia commonly occurs where chronic tissue damage is followed by extensive regeneration. For example, squamous metaplasia of the bronchi occurs when the ciliated respiratory epithelial cells of people who smoke develop into squamous, or flattened, cells. In intestinal metaplasia of the stomach, patches resembling intestinal tissue arise in the gastric mucosa, often in association with gastric ulcers. Both of these types of metaplasia may progress to cancer.

Anaplasia is a loss of visible differentiation that can occur in advanced cancer. In general, early cancers resemble their tissue of origin and are described and classified by their pattern of differentiation. However, as they develop, they produce variants of more abnormal appearance and increased malignancy. Finally, a highly anaplastic growth can occur, in which the cancerous cells bear no visible relation to the parent tissue.

CELL DEATH

There are two major types of cell death: necrosis and apoptosis. These two pathways, imposed from without (necrosis) or programmed from within (apoptosis), have different morphological features and involve different intracellular mechanisms. The detailed study of these mechanisms was a relatively recent development in science, having gained significant interest only in the mid-to-late-20th century. The concept of cell death, however, is quite old. Indeed, the first use of the term *apoptosis* in the context of medicine dates from the 4th century BCE and is ascribed to Greek physician Hippocrates. The term was used to describe the localized tissue death associated with gangrene, a disease caused by prolonged interruption of blood flow to tissues. The specific type of tissue death observed in gangrene is now understood to occur as a result of necrosis, not apoptosis. Hippocrates, however, had no way of knowing the difference between the two, based on the ways in which these terms are now distinguished in modern science. In fact, apoptosis is derived from a Greek word used to describe the phenomenon of leaf fall from plants. In contrast, the term *necrosis* is derived from the Greek nekrōsis, meaning "death." Thus, the ancient Greeks recognized the two as being different, but only on the scale of whole organisms, as opposed to individual cells. In 1972 apoptosis found meaning in modern science, being used to describe a distinct "programmed" mechanism of cell death. The subsequent elucidation of the cellular pathways underlying apoptosis enabled scientists to clearly distinguish this form of cell death from necrosis, something that had for many years caused confusion in cell biology and in medicine.

NECROSIS

Necrosis is cell death involving a circumscribed area of plant or animal tissue that occurs as a result of an outside agent. Necrosis may follow a wide variety of injuries, both physical (cuts, burns, bruises) and biological (effects of disease-causing agents). The sign of necrosis—dead tissue—is called a lesion, and it is often of diagnostic value. Necrosis is characterized by early swelling of the cytoplasm and of the mitochondria within it. Later changes include the appearance of localized densities, possibly related to calcium deposition, in the matrix (ground substance) of the mitochondria. This is followed by the dissolution of other cytoplasmic organelles and the separation of affected cells from their neighbors through shearing of intercellular junctions. Nuclear alterations occur late and are relatively unremarkable. The nucleus swells, becomes darker (pyknosis), and ruptures (karyolysis) at about the same time as does the cell membrane.

The basic mechanism of necrosis is thought to be a loss of control over cell volume, related to changes in the permeability of the cell membrane.

These changes form the basis of several of the tests used to diagnose a necrotic cell in the laboratory. The affected membrane rapidly loses its ion-pumping capacity, and there are dramatic increases in the intracellular concentrations of sodium and calcium ions. This is followed by osmotic shock and the development of intracellular acidosis. The early injury to the mitochondria has profound repercussions on intracellular oxidative metabolism. The point of no return is reached with irreversible damage to mito-chondrial structure and function. Later still, the lyso-somes rupture, releasing their acid enzymes into the cytoplasm of the cell. This produces an ionic milieu unsuitable to the survival of the nucleus. Loss of the cell's capacity to synthesize protein is the ultimate proof that it is functionally dead.

APOPTOSIS

Apoptosis, or programmed cell death, is a mecha-nism that allows cells to self-destruct when stimu-lated by the appropriate trigger. Apoptosis is initi-ated for various reasons, such as when a cell is no longer needed within the body or when it becomes a threat to the health of the organism. Apoptosis is necessary in embryonic development as well as in the daily maintenance of a mature organism. The aberrant inhibition or initiation of apoptosis contrib-utes to many disease processes, including cancer.

Embryologists in the early 20th century were familiar with the process of programmed cell death. They observed that as an embryo develops, many of its cells are sacrificed to create the final form of the organism. Not until 1972, however, did researchers John F.R. Kerr, Andrew H. Wyllie, and Alastair Currie recognize the broader significance of this mechanism. They coined the term *apoptosis* from the Greek word meaning "falling off," as leaves do in autumn, to describe this natural, timely death of cells.

Apoptosis is a normal physiological process that offsets cell proliferation. It is a genetically programmed event that can be set in motion by a variety of internal or external stimuli. A signal activates genes in the cell's suicide pathway, which encode the proteins that destroy the cell's structural proteins and genetic material. A number of morphological changes occur in the apoptotic cell— for example, the cell begins to shrivel and pull away from other cells, bubblelike formations appear on its surface, and chromatin (chromosomal DNA and protein) in the cell's nucleus condenses. The cell then either is consumed by other cells or breaks up into smaller pieces that are engulfed by scavenger cells. Cells in virtually all tissues may be sacrificed through apoptosis for the good of the organism. For example, the cells of the uterine wall undergo programmed death in the monthly menstrual cycle.

Various phenomena can disturb the regulation of the cell death pathway, causing too many or too few cells to die. Many types of disease result from such disruptions. If, for example, a mutation occurs in a gene that induces apoptosis, such as the tumour-suppressor gene *TP53*, which encodes a protein called p53, the cell that harbours the gene may fail to respond to the cue to die. As a result the cell may proliferate uncontrollably and form a cancerous tumour. In other cases a virus may interfere with the regulation of apoptosis, inducing healthy cells to die. This mechanism is believed to play a role in AIDS, the disease in which infection with HIV (human immunodeficiency virus) results in the destruction of healthy white blood cells called T lymphocytes.

CANCER DEVELOPMENT

Many cells undergo programmed cell death during fetal development. Apoptosis also may occur when a cell becomes damaged or deregulated, as is the case during tumour development and other pathological processes. Thus, when functioning properly, the body can induce apoptosis to rid itself of cancer cells.

Not all cancer cells succumb in this manner, however. Some find ways to escape apoptosis. Two mutations identified in human tumours lead to a loss of programmed cell death. One mutation inactivates the p53 protein, which normally can trigger apoptosis.

The second mutation affects a proto-oncogene called *BCL-2*, which codes for a protein that blocks cell suicide. When mutated, the *BCL-2* gene produces excessive amounts of the Bcl-2 protein, which prevents the apoptosis program from being activated. Malignant lymphomas that stem from B lymphocytes exhibit this *BCL-2* behaviour. The alteration of the *BCL-2* gene is caused by a chromosomal translocation that keeps the gene in a permanent "on" position. Loss of p53 function protects cells from only certain kinds of suicide, whereas the overproduction of Bcl-2 completely blocks access to apoptosis.

The blocking of apoptosis is thought to be an important mechanism in tumour generation. This mutation also may contribute to the development of tumours that are resistant to radiation and drug therapies, most of which destroy cancer cells by inducing apoptosis in them. If some cells within a tumour are unable to commit suicide, they will survive treatment and proliferate, creating a tumour refractory to therapy of this type. In this way apoptosis-inducing therapies may actually select for cancer cells resistant to apoptosis.

TELOMERASE

Immortalization is another way that cells escape death. Normal cells have a limited capacity to replicate, and so they age and die. The processes of aging and dying are regulated in part by DNA segments called telomeres, which are found at the ends of chromosomes. Telomeres shorten every time chromosomes are replicated and the cell divides. Once they have been reduced to a certain size, the cell reaches a crisis point, is prevented from dividing further, and dies.

This form of growth control appears to be inactivated by oncogenic expression or tumour suppression activity. In cells undergoing malignant transformation, telomeres do shorten, but, as the crisis point nears, a formerly inactive enzyme called telomerase becomes activated. This enzyme prevents the telomeres from shortening further and thereby prolongs the life of the cell.

Most malignant tumours—including breast, colon, prostate, and ovarian cancers—exhibit telomerase activity, and the more advanced the cancer, the greater the frequency of detectable telomerase in independent samples. If cell immortality contributes to the growth of most cancers, telomerase would appear to be an attractive target for therapy.

CELL THEORY AND RESEARCH

The study of cells as fundamental units of living things forms the basis of the field known as cell biology. The earliest phase of cell study began with English scientist Robert Hooke's microscopic investigations of cork and his introduction of the term *cell* in 1665. In the 19th century two Germans, the botanist Matthias Schleiden and the biologist Theodor Schwann, were among the first to clearly state that cells are the fundamental particles of both plants and animals. This pronouncement—the cell theory—was amply confirmed and elaborated by a series of discoveries and interpretations.

In 1892 the German embryologist and anatomist Oscar Hertwig suggested that organism processes are reflections of cellular processes. His work established cytology (now generally referred to as cell biology) as a separate branch of biology. Research into the activities of chromosomes led to the founding of cytogenetics, in 1902–04, when the American geneticist Walter Sutton and the German zoologist Theodor Boveri demonstrated the connection between cell division and heredity.

Modern cell biologists have adapted many methods of physics and chemistry to investigate cellular events. Improvements in techniques for growing cells in the laboratory have revolutionized science and medicine. For example, scientists now can build "bioartificial" tissues for transplantation into patients and are able to investigate individual steps in the process of cell differentiation. These developments have important implications in medicine, specifically for the regeneration of tissue in persons affected by certain diseases.

THE HISTORY OF CELL THEORY

Although the microscopists of the 17th century had made detailed descriptions of plant and animal structure and Hooke had coined the term *cell*, their observations lacked an underlying theoretical unity. It was not until 1838 that Schleiden, in his studies of plant anatomy, stated, "the lower plants all consist of one cell, while the higher ones are composed of (many) individual cells." When Schwann extended the cellular theory to include animals, he thereby unified botany and zoology. The formation of the cell theory—all plants and animals are made up of cells—marked a great conceptual advance in biology, and it resulted in renewed attention to the living processes that take place within cells.

EARLY OBSERVATIONS

The history of cell theory is a history of the actual observation of cells, because early prediction and speculation about the nature of the cell were generally unsuccessful. The decisive event that allowed the observation of cells was the invention of the microscope in the 17th century, after which interest in the "invisible" world was stimulated. Even after Hooke's investigations of cork in 1665 and after the publication in 1672 of excellent pictures of plant tissues, no significance was attached to the contents within the cell walls. The magnifying powers of the microscope and the inadequacy of techniques for preparing cells for observation precluded a study of the intimate details of the cell contents. The inspired Dutch microscopist Antonie van Leeuwenhoek, beginning in 1673, discovered blood cells, spermatozoa, and a lively world of "animalcules." A new world of unicellular organisms was opened up. Such discoveries extended the known variety of living things but did not bring insight into their basic uniformity. Moreover, when van Leeuwenhoek observed the

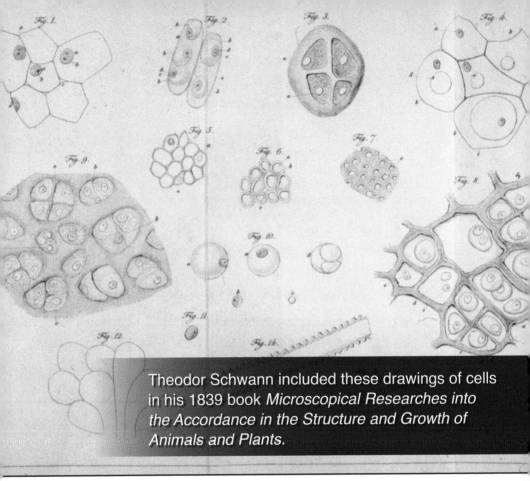

Theodor Schwann included these drawings of cells in his 1839 book *Microscopical Researches into the Accordance in the Structure and Growth of Animals and Plants.*

swarming of his animalcules but failed to observe their division, he could only reinforce the idea that they arose spontaneously.

Cell theory was not formulated for nearly 200 years after the introduction of microscopy. Explanations for this delay range from the poor quality of the microscopes to the persistence of ancient ideas concerning the definition of a fundamental living unit. Many observations of cells were made, but apparently none of the observers were able to assert forcefully that cells are the units of biological structure and function.

Three critical discoveries made during the 1830s, when improved microscopes with suitable lenses, higher powers of magnification without aberration, and more satisfactory illumination became available, were decisive events in the early development of cell theory. First, the nucleus was observed by Scottish botanist Robert Brown in 1833 as a constant component of plant cells. Next, nuclei were also observed and recognized as such in some animal cells. Finally, a living substance called protoplasm was recognized within cells, its vitality made evident by its active streaming, or flowing, movements, especially in plant cells. After these three discoveries, cells, previously considered as mere pores in plant tissue, could no longer be thought of as empty, because they contained living material.

Schwann and Schleiden clearly stated in 1839 that cells are the "elementary particles of organisms" in both plants and animals and recognized that some organisms are unicellular and others multicellular. This statement was made in Schwann's *Mikroskopische Untersuchungen über die Übereinstimmung in der Struktur und dem Wachstume der Tiere und Pflanzen* (1839; *Microscopical Researches into the Accordance in the Structure and Growth of Animals and Plants*). Schleiden's contributions on plants were acknowledged by Schwann as the basis for his comparison of animal and plant structure.

Schleiden and Schwann's descriptive statements concerning the cellular basis of biologic structure are straightforward and acceptable to modern thought. They recognized the common features of cells to be the membrane, nucleus, and cell body and described them in comparisons of various animal and plant tissues. A statement by Schleiden pointed toward the future direction of cell studies:

Each cell leads a double life: an independent one, pertaining to its own development alone; and another incidental, insofar as it has become an integral part of a plant. It is, however, easy to perceive that the vital process of the individual cells must form the first, absolutely indispensable fundamental basis, both as regards vegetable physiology and comparative physiology in general.

Schwann and Schleiden were not alone in contributing to this great generalization of natural science, for strong intimations of the cell theory occur in the work of their predecessors. Recognizing that the basic problem was the origin of cells, these early investigators invented a hypothesis of "free cell formation," according to which cells developed de novo out of an unformed substance, a "cytoblastema," by a sequence of events in which first the nucleolus develops, followed by the nucleus, the cell body, and finally the cell membrane. The best physical model of the generation of formed bodies then available was crystallization, and their theory was inspired by that model. In retrospect, the hypothesis of free cell formation would not seem to have been justified, however, because cell division, a feature not characteristic of crystallization processes, had frequently been observed by earlier microscopists, especially among single-celled organisms. Even though cell division was observed repeatedly in the following decades, the theory of free cell formation lingered throughout most of the 19th century. However, it came to be thought of more and more as a possible exception to the general principle of the reproduction of cells by division. The correct general principle was affirmed in 1855 by a German pathologist and statesman, Rudolf Virchow, who asserted that *omnis cellula e cellula* ("all cells come from cells").

The inherently complex events of cell division prevented a quick resolution of the complete sequence of changes that occur during the process. First, it was noted that a cell with a nucleus divides into two cells, each having a nucleus. Hence, it was concluded that the nucleus must divide, and direct division of nuclei was duly described by some. Better techniques served to create perplexity, because it was found that during cell division the nucleus as such disappears. Moreover, at the time of division, dimly discerned masses, now recognized as chromosomes, were seen to appear temporarily. Observations in the 1870s culminated in the highly accurate description and interpretation of cell division by German anatomist Walther Flemming in 1882. His advanced techniques of fixing and staining cells enabled him to see that cell reproduction involves the transmission of chromosomes from the parent to daughter cells by the process of mitosis and that the division of the cell body is the terminal event of that reproduction.

The discovery that the number of chromosomes remains constant from one generation to the next resulted in the full description of the process of meiosis. The description of meiosis, combined with the observation that fertilization is fundamentally the union of maternal and paternal sets of chromosomes, culminated in the understanding of the physical basis of reproduction and heredity. Meiosis and fertilization therefore came to be understood as the complementary events in the life cycle of organisms: Meiosis halves the number of chromosomes in the formation of spores (plants) or gametes (animals), while fertilization restores the number through the union of gametes. By the 1890s "life" in all of its manifestations could be thought of as an expression of cells.

THE PROTOPLASM CONCEPT

As the concept of the cell as the elementary particle of life developed during the 19th century, it was paralleled by the protoplasm concept—the idea that the protoplasm within the cell is responsible for life. Protoplasm had been defined in 1835 as the ground substance of living material and hence responsible for all living processes. That life is an activity of an elementary particle, the cell, can be contrasted with the view that it is the expression of a living complex substance—even a supermolecule—called a protoplasm. The protoplasm concept was supported by observations of the streaming movements of the apparently slimy contents of living cells.

Advocates of the protoplasm concept implied that cells were either fragments or containers of protoplasm. Suspicious and often contemptuous of information obtained from dead and stained cells, such researchers discovered most of the basic information on the physical properties—mechanical, optical, electrical, and contractile—of the living cell.

An assessment of the usefulness of the concept of protoplasm is difficult. It was not wholly false. On the one hand, it encouraged the study of the chemical and mechanical properties of cell contents. On the other hand, it also generated a resistance, evident as late as the 1930s, to the development of biochemical techniques for cell fractionation and to the realization that large molecules (macromolecules) are important cellular constituents. As the cell has become fractionated into its component parts, protoplasm, as a term, no longer has meaning. The word protoplasm is still used, however, in describing the phenomenon of protoplasmic streaming—the phenomenon from which the concept of protoplasm originally emerged.

CONTRIBUTION OF OTHER SCIENCES

Appreciation of the cell as the unit of life has accrued from important sources other than microscopy. Perhaps the most important is microbiology. Even though the small size of microorganisms prohibited much observation of their detailed structure until the advent of electron microscopy, they could be grown easily and rapidly. Thus it was that French chemist and microbiologist Louis Pasteur's studies of microbes published in 1861 helped to establish the principle of biogenesis—namely, that organisms arise only by the reproduction of other organisms. Fundamental ideas regarding the metabolic attributes of cells—their ability to transform simple nutritional substances into cell substance and usable energy—came from microbiology. Pasteur perhaps overplayed the relation between catalysis and the living state of cells in considering enzymatic action to be an attribute of the living cell rather than of the catalytic molecules (enzymes) contained in the cell. It is a fact, however, that much of cell chemistry is enzyme chemistry—and that enzymes are one defining attribute of cells. The techniques of microbiology eventually opened the way for microbial genetics, which in turn provided the means for solving the fundamental problems of molecular biology that were inaccessible at first to direct attack by biochemical methods.

The science of molecular biology would be most capable of overthrowing the cell theory if the latter were an exaggerated generalization. On the contrary, molecular biology has become the foundation of cell science, for it has demonstrated not only that basic processes such as the genetic code and protein synthesis are similar in all living systems but also that they are made possible by the same cell components (e.g., chromosomes, ribosomes, and membranes).

In the overlapping histories of cell biology and medicine, two events are especially important. First, the identification in 1827 by Prussian-Estonian embryologist Karl Ernst Ritter von Baer of the ovum (unfertilized egg) as a cell was important considering the many ways it often differs from other cells. Baer not only laid the foundations for reproductive biology but also provided important evidence for the cell theory at a critical time. The second important event was the promotion in 1855 of the concept of cellular pathology by Virchow. His idea that human diseases are diseases of cells and can be identified and understood as such gave an authority to cell theory.

Although biochemistry might have made considerable progress without cell theory, each influenced the other almost from the start. When it was established that most biochemical phenomena are shared by all cells, the cell could be defined by its metabolism as well as by its structure. Cytochemistry, or histochemistry, made a brilliant start in 1869, when Swiss biochemist Johann Friedrich Miescher postulated that the nucleus must have a characteristic chemistry and then went on to discover nucleic acids, which have since been shown to be the crucial molecules of inheritance and metabolism.

Cell theory alone cannot explain the development and unity of the multicellular organism. A cell is not necessarily an independently functioning unit, and a plant or an animal is not merely an accumulation of individual cells. Fortunately, however, the long controversy centring upon the individuality and separateness of cells has ended. Cell biology now focuses on the interactions and communication among cells as well as on the analysis of the single cell. The influence of the environment on the cell has always been considered important, and now it is recognized too that one important part of the environment of a cell is other cells.

Cell theory thus is not so comprehensive as to eliminate the concept of the organism as more than the sum of its parts. But the study of a particular organism requires the investigation of cells both as individuals and as groups. The problem of cancer is an example: A plant or animal governs the division of its own cells. The right cells must divide, be differentiated, and then be integrated into the proper organ system at the right time and place. Breakdown results in a variety of abnormalities, one of which is cancer. When the cell biologist studies the problem of the regulation of cell division, the ultimate objective is to understand the effect of the whole organism on an individual cell.

TISSUE CULTURE

Cell culture and tissue culture are methods of biological research in which cells or fragments of tissue from an animal or plant are transferred to an artificial environment in which they can continue to survive and function. The cultured entity may consist of a single cell, a population of cells, or a whole or part of an organ. Cells in culture may multiply; change size, form, or function; exhibit specialized activity (muscle cells, for example, may contract); or interact with other cells.

Tissue culture is a relatively recent development. In 1907 American zoologist Ross G. Harrison successfully demonstrated the growth of frog nerve cell processes in a medium of clotted lymph. Thereafter, a number of experimenters succeeded in cultivating animal cells, using as culture media a variety of biological fluids, such as lymph, blood serum, plasma, and tissue extracts.

Tissue culture permits control of the cellular environment, allowing the behaviour of cells to be both examined and manipulated. Tissue cultures have revealed basic information about cells regarding their composition and form; their biochemical, genetic, and reproductive activity; their nutrition, metabolism, specialized functions, and processes of aging and healing; the effects on cells of physical, chemical, and biological agents (drugs and viruses, for example); and the differences between normal cells and abnormal cells such as cancers. Work with tissue cultures has helped identify infections, enzyme deficiencies, and chromosomal abnormalities; classify brain tumours; and formulate and test drugs and vaccines.

Cells may be grown in a culture medium of biological origin such as blood serum or tissue extract, in a chemically defined synthetic medium, or in a mixture of the two. A medium must contain proper proportions of the necessary nutrients for the cells to be studied and must be appropriately acid or alkaline. Cultures are usually grown either as single layers of cells on a glass or plastic surface or as a suspension in a liquid or semisolid medium. To initiate a culture, a tiny sample of the tissue is dispersed on or in the medium, and the flask, tube, or plate containing the culture is then incubated, usually at a temperature close to that of the tissue's normal environment. Sterile conditions are maintained to prevent contamination with microorganisms.

Live cultured cells may be examined directly with a microscope or observed by means of photographs and motion pictures taken through the microscope. Cells may also be killed, preserved, and stained for further examination or cut into thin sections to disclose additional details under a light or electron microscope. Cells in tissue culture are subjected to a broad range of experimental treatment. For example, viruses, drugs, hormones, vitamins, disease-causing microorganisms, or suspected cancer-producing chemicals may be added to the culture. Sometimes cultures are grown from single cells, producing uniform biological populations called clones.

Cultures have been used to investigate fundamental processes of growth and development in both normal and abnormal tissues. One finding has been that normal cells undergo an aging process, retaining their ability to multiply readily for only 50 to 100 generations, after which the rate decreases markedly. Many cancer cells, on the other hand, apparently can be perpetuated forever.

Since the discovery that certain viruses will grow in tissue cultures, the technique has been used to produce vaccines against poliomyelitis, influenza, measles, mumps, and other infectious diseases. Cell cultures have also produced viral inhibitors, including interferon. Hormones are produced from

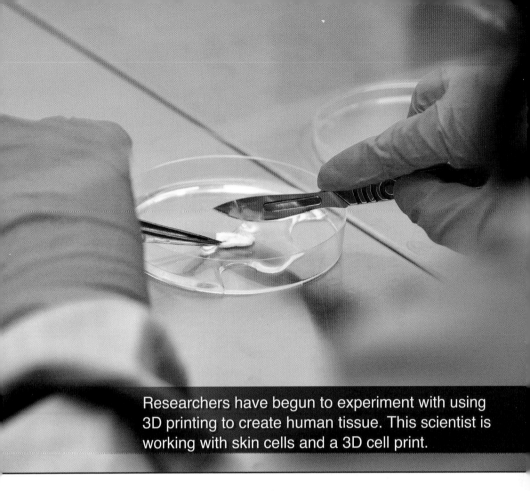

Researchers have begun to experiment with using 3D printing to create human tissue. This scientist is working with skin cells and a 3D cell print.

cultures of cells or organs. The cultured white blood cells from two individuals can be used to determine compatibility between potential donors and recipients of tissue transplants. By removing and culturing cells from a pregnant woman, it is possible to tell whether her fetus has the chromosome defect associated with Down syndrome.

The identification and diagnosis of chromosome abnormalities and inherited disorders has been greatly enhanced by the development of somatic cell genetics. Tissue culture techniques have been used to culture many kinds of hybrid cells that contain chromosomes from different species in the same cell, allowing the functions of individual chromosomes to be separately defined. Tissue culture studies have clarified the genetic causes of certain hereditary diseases, and methods have been developed for detecting environmental substances that may cause gene damage. The nature of certain cancers has been elucidated by the discovery of specific genes and chromosomal aberrations that are associated with the disease. Studies of cell cultures have revealed the existence of a so-called cytoskeleton in mammalian cells, which gives the cell its shape and regulates a variety of biochemical activities. The methods of somatic cell genetics are applied to plant cells in an effort to develop new strains of cereal crops with improved nutritional properties.

CRYOPRESERVATION

Cells and tissues are commonly preserved by freezing, or cryopreservation. Cryopreservation is based on the ability of certain small molecules to enter cells and prevent dehydration and formation of intracellular ice crystals, which can cause cell death and destruction of cell organelles during the freezing process. Two common cryoprotective agents are dimethyl sulfoxide (DMSO) and glycerol. Glycerol is used primarily for cryoprotection of red blood cells, and DMSO is used for protection of most other cells and tissues. A sugar called trehalose, which occurs in organisms capable of surviving extreme dehydration, is used for freeze-drying methods of cryopreservation. Trehalose stabilizes cell membranes, and it is particularly useful for the preservation of sperm, stem cells, and blood cells.

Most systems of cellular cryopreservation use a controlled-rate freezer. This freezing system delivers liquid nitrogen into a closed chamber into which the cell suspension is placed. Careful monitoring of the rate of freezing helps to prevent rapid cellular dehydration and ice-crystal formation. In general, the cells are taken from room temperature to approximately -90 °C (-130 °F) in a controlled-rate freezer. The frozen cell suspension is then transferred into a liquid-nitrogen freezer maintained at extremely cold temperatures with nitrogen in either the vapour or the liquid phase. Cryopreservation based on freeze-drying does not require use of liquid-nitrogen freezers.

An important application of cryopreservation is in the freezing and storage of hematopoietic stem cells, which are found in the bone marrow and peripheral blood. In autologous bone-marrow rescue, hematopoietic stem cells are collected from a patient's bone marrow prior to treatment with high-dose chemotherapy. Following treatment, the patient's cryopreserved cells are thawed and infused back into the body. This procedure is necessary, since high-dose chemotherapy is extremely toxic to the bone marrow. The ability to cryopreserve hematopoietic stem cells has greatly enhanced the outcome for the treatment of certain lymphomas and solid tumour malignancies. In the case of patients with leukemia, their blood cells are cancerous and cannot be used for autologous bone-marrow rescue. As a result, these patients rely on cryopreserved blood collected from the umbilical cords of newborn infants or on cryopreserved hematopoietic stem cells obtained from donors. Since the late 1990s it has been recognized that hematopoietic stem cells and mesenchymal stem cells (derived from embryonic connective tissue) are capable of differentiating into skeletal and cardiac muscle tissues, nerve tissue, and bone. Today there is intense interest in the growth of these cells in tissue culture systems, as well as in the cryopreservation of these cells for future therapy for a wide variety of disorders, including disorders of the nervous and muscle systems and diseases of the liver and heart.

Profound hypothermia is a form of mild cryopreservation used in human patients that enables living tissues to be protected from stress and other forms of damage as a result of certain medical procedures. A common use of induction of profound hypothermia is for complex cardiovascular surgical procedures. After the patient has been placed on complete cardiopulmonary bypass, using a heart-lung machine, the blood passes through a cooling chamber. Controlled cooling of the patient may reach extremely low temperatures of around 10–14 °C (50–57 °F). This amount of cooling effectively stops all cerebral activity and provides protection for all the vital organs. When this extreme cooling has been achieved, the heartlung machine can be stopped, and the surgeon can correct very complex aortic and cardiac defects during circulatory arrest. During this time, no blood is circulating within the patient. After the surgery has been completed, the blood is gradually warmed in the same heat exchanger used for cooling. Gradual warming back to normal body temperatures results in resumption of normal brain and organ functions. This profound hypothermia, however, is far removed from freezing and long-term cryopreservation.

Cells can live more than a decade if properly frozen. In addition, certain tissues, such as parathyroid glands, veins, cardiac valves, and aortic tissue, can be successfully cryopreserved. Freezing is also used to store and maintain long-term viability of early human embryos, ova (eggs), and sperm. The freezing procedures used for these tissues are well established, and, in the presence of cryoprotective agents, the tissues can be stored over long periods of time at temperatures of -14 °C (6.8 °F). Research has shown that whole animals frozen in the absence of cryoprotective agents can yield viable cells containing intact DNA upon thawing. For example, nuclei of brain cells from whole mice stored at -20 °C (-4 °F) for more than 15 years have been used to generate lines of embryonic stem cells. These cells were subsequently used to produce mouse clones.

TISSUE ENGINEERING

Cell biology plays a fundamental role in helping scientists to achieve a better understanding of human disease and in developing new therapies for medicine. Fields such as tissue engineering and regenerative medicine have presented opportunities for the development of tissues to replace those damaged by injury or disease.

Tissue engineering is a scientific field concerned with the development of biological substitutes capable of replacing diseased or damaged tissue in humans. The term *tissue engineering* was introduced in the late 1980s. By the early 1990s the concept of applying engineering to the repair of biological tissue resulted in the rapid growth of tissue engineering as an interdisciplinary field with the potential to revolutionize important areas of medicine.

Tissue engineering integrates biological components, such as cells and growth factors, with engineering principles and synthetic materials. Substitute tissues can be produced by first seeding human cells onto scaffolds, which may be made from collagen or from a biodegradable polymer. The scaffolds are then incubated in mediums containing growth factors, which stimulate the cells to grow and divide. As cells spread across the scaffold, the substitute tissue is formed. This tissue can be implanted into the human body, with the implanted scaffold eventually being either absorbed or dissolved.

Examples of tissues that are candidates for tissue engineering include skin, cartilage, heart, and bone. The production of skin substitutes has played an important role in improving the success of skin graft surgeries, especially for complex wounds such as burns. Substitute tissues of the renal system, including urinary bladders and urethras, have also been engineered and transplanted successfully, thereby broadening therapeutic opportunities for complicated renal disorders. Scaffolds and bioartificial tissues are being investigated for their use in the development of functioning bioartificial limbs; the first such limb to be successfully developed—a rat leg with functioning muscles and veins—was reported in 2015.

STEM CELLS

A stem cell is an undifferentiated cell that can divide to produce some offspring cells that continue as stem cells and some cells that are destined to differentiate. Stem cells are an ongoing source of the differentiated cells that make up the tissues and organs of animals and plants. There is great interest in stem cells because they have potential in the development of therapies for replacing defective or damaged cells resulting from a variety of disorders and injuries, such as Parkinson disease, heart disease, and diabetes. There are two major types of stem cells: embryonic stem cells and adult stem cells, which are also called tissue stem cells. However, the way in which these cells are acquired and utilized has been a source of controversy, and debates over which embryonic stem cell lines (generations of cells originating from the same group of parent cells) researchers are permitted to study has hindered progress in the field of regenerative medicine.

EMBRYONIC STEM CELLS

Embryonic stem cells (often referred to as ES cells) are stem cells that are derived from the inner cell mass of a mammalian embryo at a very early stage of development, when it is composed of a hollow sphere of dividing cells (a blastocyst). Embryonic stem cells from human embryos and from embryos of certain other mammalian species can be grown in tissue culture.

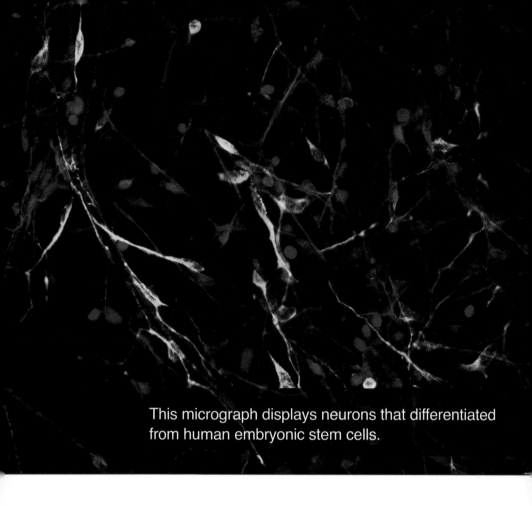

This micrograph displays neurons that differentiated from human embryonic stem cells.

MOUSE EMBRYONIC STEM CELLS

The most-studied embryonic stem cells are mouse embryonic stem cells, which were first reported in 1981. This type of stem cell can be cultured indefinitely in the presence of leukemia inhibitory factor (LIF), a glycoprotein cytokine. If cultured mouse embryonic stem cells are injected into an early mouse embryo at the blastocyst stage, they will become integrated into the embryo and produce cells that differentiate into most or all of the tissue types that subsequently develop. This ability to repopulate mouse embryos is the key defining feature of embryonic stem cells, and because of it they are considered to be pluripotent—able to give rise to any cell type of the adult organism. If the embryonic stem cells are kept in culture in the absence of LIF, they will differentiate into "embryoid bodies," which somewhat resemble early mouse embryos at the egg-cylinder stage, with embryonic stem cells inside an outer layer of endoderm. If embryonic stem cells are grafted into an adult mouse, they will develop into a type of tumour called a teratoma, which contains a variety of differentiated tissue types.

Mouse embryonic stem cells are widely used to create genetically modified mice. This is done by introducing new genes into embryonic stem cells in tissue culture, selecting the particular genetic variant that is desired, and then inserting the genetically modified cells into mouse embryos. The resulting chimeric mice are composed partly of host cells and partly of the donor embryonic stem cells. As long as some of the chimeric mice have germ cells (sperm or eggs) that have been derived from the embryonic stem cells, it is possible to breed a line of mice that have the same genetic constitution as the embryonic stem cells and therefore incorporate the genetic modification that was made in vitro. This method has been used to produce thousands of new genetic lines of mice. In many such genetic lines, individual genes have been ablated in order to study their biological function. In others, genes have been introduced that have the same mutations that are found in various human genetic diseases. These mouse models for human disease are used in research to investigate both the pathology of the disease and new methods for therapy.

HUMAN EMBRYONIC STEM CELLS

Extensive experience with mouse embryonic stem cells made it possible for scientists to grow human embryonic stem cells from early human embryos, and the first human stem cell line was created in 1998. Human embryonic stem cells are in many respects similar to mouse embryonic stem cells, but they do not require LIF for their maintenance. The human embryonic stem cells form a wide variety of differentiated tissues in vitro, and they form terato-mas when grafted into immunosuppressed mice. It is not known whether the cells can colonize all the tissues of a human embryo, but it is presumed from their other properties that they are indeed pluripo-tent cells, and they therefore are regarded as a pos-sible source of differentiated cells for cell therapy—the replacement of a patient's defective cell type with healthy cells. Large quantities of cells, such as dopamine-secreting neurons for the treatment of Parkinson disease and insulin-secreting pancreatic beta cells for the treatment of diabetes, could be produced from embryonic stem cells for cell transplantation. Cells for this purpose have previously been obtainable only from sources in very limited supply, such as the pancreatic beta cells obtained from the cadavers of human organ donors.

The use of human embryonic stem cells evokes ethical concerns, because the blastocyst-stage embryos are destroyed in the process of obtaining the stem cells. The embryos from which stem cells have been obtained are produced through in vitro fertilization, and people who consider preimplantation human embryos to be human beings generally believe that such work is morally wrong. Others accept it because they regard the blastocysts to be simply balls of cells, and human cells used in laboratories have not previously been accorded any special moral or legal status. Moreover, it is known that none of the cells of the inner cell mass are exclusively destined to become part of the embryo itself—all of the cells contribute some or all of their cell offspring to the placenta, which also has not been accorded any special legal status. The divergence of views on this issue is illustrated by the fact that the use of human embryonic stem cells is allowed in some countries and prohibited in others.

In 2009 the U.S. Food and Drug Administration approved the first clinical trial designed to test a human embryonic stem cell-based therapy, but the trial was halted in late 2011 because of a lack of funding and a change in lead American biotech company Geron's business directives. The therapy to be tested was known as GRNOPC1, which consisted of progenitor cells (partially differentiated cells) that, once inside the body, matured into neural cells known as oligodendrocytes. The oligodendrocyte progenitors of GRNOPC1 were derived from human embryonic stem cells. The therapy was designed for the restoration of nerve function in persons suffering from acute spinal cord injury.

EMBRYONIC GERM CELLS

Embryonic germ (EG) cells, derived from primordial germ cells found in the gonadal ridge of a late embryo, have many of the properties of embryonic stem cells. The primordial germ cells in an embryo develop into stem cells that in an adult generate the reproductive gametes (sperm or eggs). In mice and humans it is possible to grow embryonic germ cells in tissue culture with the appropriate growth factors—namely, LIF and another cytokine called fibroblast growth factor.

ADULT STEM CELLS

Some tissues in the adult body, such as the epidermis of the skin, the lining of the small intestine, and bone marrow, undergo continuous cellular turnover. They contain stem cells, which persist indefinitely, and a much larger number of transit amplifying cells, which arise from the stem cells and divide a finite number of times until they become differentiated. The stem cells exist in niches formed by other cells, which secrete substances that keep the stem cells alive and active. Some types of tissue, such as liver tissue, show minimal cell division or undergo cell division only when injured. In such tissues there is probably no special stem cell population, and any cell can participate in tissue regeneration when required.

EPITHELIAL STEM CELLS

The epidermis of the skin contains layers of cells called keratinocytes. Only the basal layer, next to the dermis, contains cells that divide. A number of these cells are stem cells, but the majority are transit amplifying cells. The keratinocytes slowly move outward through the epidermis as they mature, and they eventually die and are sloughed off at the surface of the skin. The epithelium of the small intestine forms projections called villi, which are interspersed with small pits called crypts. The dividing cells are located in the crypts, with the stem cells lying near the base of each crypt. Cells are continuously produced in the crypts, migrate onto the villi, and are eventually shed into the lumen of the intestine. As they migrate, they differentiate into the cell types characteristic of the intestinal epithelium.

DISCOVERING PLURIPOTENCY IN MATURE CELLS

British developmental biologist John B. Gurdon (1933–) and Japanese physician and researcher Shinya Yamanaka (1962–) shared the 2012 Nobel Prize for Physiology or Medicine for the discovery that mature cells could be reprogrammed.

Gurdon was the first to demonstrate that egg cells are able to reprogram differentiated (mature) cell nuclei, reverting them to a pluripotent state, in which they regain the capacity to become any type of cell. Gurdon's work ultimately came to form the foundation for major advances in cloning and stem cell research, including the generation of Dolly—the first successfully cloned mammal—by British developmental biologist Sir Ian Wilmut, as well as Yamanaka's discovery of induced pluripotent stem (iPS) cells, which revolutionized the field of regenerative medicine.

In 1956 Gurdon began his graduate studies in zoology in the laboratory of embryologist Michail Fischberg and initiated a series of experiments on nuclear transfer (the introduction of the nucleus from a differentiated cell into an egg cell that had its own nucleus removed) in the African clawed frog (*Xenopus laevis*). He proceeded to generate cloned tadpoles from differentiated *Xenopus* intestinal cell nuclei, demonstrating that egg cells could undifferentiate previously differentiated nuclei and that normal embryos could be produced with the technique. He published his

(Continued on the next page)

(Continued from the previous page)

seminal findings in 1958. However, because American scientists Robert Briggs and Thomas King previously had found that the transfer of nuclei from partially differentiated cells consistently resulted in the production of abnormal embryos in the frog *Rana pipiens*, Gurdon's results were greeted with skepticism.

In 1971 Gurdon joined the Medical Research Council Laboratory of Molecular Biology (LMB) in Cambridge, where he worked to identify the molecules in egg cells that were responsible for the nuclear reprogramming effect. Also during that time, other scientists began to confirm the results of Gurdon's early experiments with *Xenopus*, which effectively solidified his position as a leader in nuclear transfer. He was knighted in 1995.

Yamanaka received an M.D. from Kōbe University in 1987 and a Ph.D. in pharmacology from the Ōsaka City University Graduate School in 1993. That year he joined the Gladstone Institute of Cardiovascular Disease, San Francisco, where he began investigating the *c-Myc* gene in different strains of knockout mice (mice in which a specific gene has been rendered nonfunctional in order to investigate the gene's function). In 2004 he moved to the Institute for Frontier Medical Sciences at Kyōto University, where he began his landmark studies on finding ways to induce pluripotency in cells. He later received funding that allowed him to split his time between Kyōto and the Gladstone Institute.

In 2006 Yamanaka announced that he had succeeded in generating iPS cells. The cells had the properties of embryonic stem cells but were produced by inserting four specific genes into the nuclei of mouse adult fibroblasts (connective-tissue cells). The following year Yamanaka reported that he had derived iPS cells from human adult fibroblasts—the first successful attempt at generating human versions of these cells. This discovery marked a turning point in stem-cell research, because it offered a way of obtaining human stem cells without the controversial use of human embryos. Yamanaka's technique to convert adult cells into iPS cells up to that time had employed a retrovirus that contained the *c-Myc* gene. This gene was believed to play a fundamental role in reprogramming the nuclei of adult cells. However, Yamanaka recognized that the activation of *c-Myc* during the process of creating iPS cells led to the formation of tumours when the stem cells were later transplanted into mice. He subsequently created iPS cells without *c-Myc* in order to render the cells non-cancerous and thereby overcome a major concern in the therapeutic safety of iPS cells. In 2008 Yamanaka reported another breakthrough—the generation of iPS cells from mouse liver and stomach cells.

BONE MARROW AND HEMATOPOIETIC STEM CELLS

Bone marrow contains cells called hematopoietic stem cells, which generate all the cell types of the blood and the immune system. Hematopoietic stem cells are also found in small numbers in peripheral blood and in larger numbers in umbilical cord blood. In bone marrow, hematopoietic stem cells are anchored to osteoblasts of the trabecular bone and to blood vessels. They generate progeny that can become lymphocytes, granulocytes, red blood cells, and certain other cell types, depending on the balance of growth factors in their immediate environment.

Work with experimental animals has shown that transplants of hematopoietic stem cells can occasionally colonize other tissues, with the transplanted cells becoming neurons, muscle cells, or epithelia. The degree to which transplanted hematopoietic stem cells are able to colonize other tissues is exceedingly small. Despite this, the use of hematopoietic stem cell transplants is being explored for conditions such as heart disease or autoimmune disorders. It is an especially attractive option for those opposed to the use of embryonic stem cells.

Bone marrow transplants (also known as bone marrow grafts) represent a type of stem cell therapy that is in common use. They are used to allow cancer patients to survive otherwise lethal doses of radiation therapy or chemotherapy that destroy the stem cells in bone marrow. For this procedure, the patient's own marrow is harvested before the cancer treatment and is then reinfused into the body after treatment. The hematopoietic stem cells of the

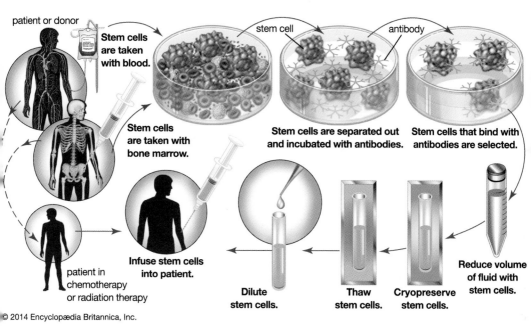

patient or donor

Stem cells are taken with blood.

stem cell

antibody

Stem cells are taken with bone marrow.

Stem cells are separated out and incubated with antibodies.

Stem cells that bind with antibodies are selected.

patient in chemotherapy or radiation therapy

Infuse stem cells into patient.

Dilute stem cells.

Thaw stem cells.

Cryopreserve stem cells.

Reduce volume of fluid with stem cells.

High doses of chemotherapy or radiation destroy not only cancer cells but also bone marrow, which is rich in blood-forming stem cells. In order to replace damaged marrow, stem cells are harvested from either the blood or the bone marrow of the cancer patient before therapy; cells also may be taken from a genetically compatible donor. In order to remove unwanted cells, such as tumour cells, from the sample, it is incubated with antibodies that bind only to stem cells. The fluid that contains the selected cells is reduced in volume and frozen until needed. The fluid is then thawed, diluted, and reinfused into the patient's body. Once in the bloodstream, the stem cells travel to the bone marrow, where they implant themselves and begin producing healthy cells.

transplant colonize the damaged marrow and eventually repopulate the blood and the immune system with functional cells. Bone marrow transplants are also often carried out between individuals (allograft). In this case the grafted marrow has some beneficial antitumour effect. Risks associated with bone marrow allografts include rejection of the graft by the patient's immune system and reaction of immune cells of the graft against the patient's tissues (graft-versus-host disease).

Bone marrow is a source for mesenchymal stem cells (sometimes called marrow stromal cells, or MSCs), which are precursors to nonhematopoietic stem cells that have the potential to differentiate into several different types of cells, including cells that form bone, muscle, and connective tissue. In cell cultures, bone-marrow-derived mesenchymal stem cells demonstrate pluripotency when exposed to substances that influence cell differentiation. Harnessing these pluripotent properties has become highly valuable in the generation of transplantable tissues and organs. In 2008 scientists used mesenchymal stem cells to bioengineer a section of trachea that was transplanted into a woman whose upper airway had been severely damaged by tuberculosis. The stem cells were derived from the woman's bone marrow, cultured in a laboratory, and used for tissue engineering. In the engineering process, a donor trachea was stripped of its interior and exterior cell linings, leaving behind a trachea scaffold of connective tissue. The stem cells derived from the recipient were then used to recolonize the interior of the scaffold, and normal epithelial cells, also isolated from the recipient, were used to recolonize the exterior of the trachea. The use of the recipient's own cells to populate the trachea scaffold prevented immune rejection and eliminated the need for immunosuppression therapy. The transplant, which was successful, was the first of its kind.

NEURAL STEM CELLS

Research has shown that there are also stem cells in the brain. In mammals very few new neurons are formed after birth, but some neurons in the olfactory bulbs and in the hippocampus are continually being formed. These neurons arise from neural stem cells, which can be cultured in vitro in the form of neurospheres—small cell clusters that contain stem cells and some of their progeny. This type of stem cell is being studied for use in cell therapy to treat Parkinson disease and other forms of neurodegeneration or traumatic damage to the central nervous system.

SOMATIC CELL NUCLEAR TRANSFER

Following experiments in animals, including those used to create Dolly the sheep, there has been much discussion about the use of somatic cell nuclear

Dolly: The Cloning of a Sheep, 1996

micropipette

cytoplasm
nucleus
DNA

egg cell
removed

adult Finn Dorset ewe

unfertilized
egg cell

nucleus removed

nucleus
donor

Finn Dorset lamb
("Dolly")

adult Scottish Blackface ewes

donor cells removed
from mammary gland

surrogate
mother

embryo
implanted

donor cells
(normal growth cycle)

enucleated
egg cell

embryo

donor cells starved

cytoplasm

nucleus   DNA

cell
fusion

low-nutrient culture medium

donor cell
(arrested growth cycle)

electrical pulses

cell
division

fertilization

egg cell
donor

Dolly the sheep was cloned using the process of somatic cell nuclear transfer (SCNT). While SCNT is used for cloning animals, it can also be used to generate embryonic stem cells. Prior to implantation of the fertilized egg into the uterus of the surrogate mother, the inner cell mass of the egg can be removed, and the cells can be grown in culture to form an embryonic stem cell line (generations of cells originating from the same group of parent cells).

transfer (SCNT) to create pluripotent human cells. In SCNT the nucleus of a somatic cell (a fully differentiated cell, excluding germ cells), which contains the majority of the cell's DNA, is removed and transferred into an unfertilized egg cell that has had its own nuclear DNA removed. The egg cell is grown in culture until it reaches the blastocyst stage. The inner cell mass is then removed from the egg, and the cells are grown in culture to form an embryonic stem cell line. These cells can then be stimulated to differentiate into various types of cells needed for transplantation. Since these cells would be genetically identical to the original donor, they could be used to treat the donor with no problems of immune rejection. Scientists generated human embryonic stem cells successfully from SCNT human embryos for the first time in 2013.

While promising, the generation and use of SCNT-derived embryonic stem cells is controversial for several reasons. One is that SCNT is inefficient, sometimes requiring dozens of eggs before one egg successfully produces embryonic stem cells. Human eggs are in short supply, and there are many legal and ethical problems associated with egg donation. There are also unknown risks involved with transplanting SCNT-derived stem cells into humans, because the mechanism by which the unfertilized egg is able to reprogram the nuclear DNA of a differentiated cell is not entirely understood. In addition, SCNT is commonly used to produce clones of animals (such as Dolly). Although the cloning of humans is currently illegal throughout the world, the egg cell that contains nuclear DNA from an adult cell could in theory be implanted into a woman's uterus and come to term as an actual cloned human. Thus, there exists strong opposition among some groups to the use of SCNT to generate human embryonic stem cells.

INDUCED PLURIPOTENT STEM CELLS

Due to the ethical and moral issues surrounding the use of embryonic stem cells, scientists have searched for ways to reprogram adult somatic cells. Studies of cell fusion, in which differentiated adult somatic cells grown in culture with embryonic stem cells fuse with the stem cells and acquire embryonic stem-cell–like properties, led to the idea that specific genes could reprogram differentiated adult cells. An advantage of cell fusion is that it relies on existing embryonic stem cells instead of eggs. However, fused cells stimulate an immune response when transplanted into humans, which leads to transplant rejection. As a result, research has become increasingly focused on the genes and proteins capable of reprogram-ming adult cells to a pluripotent state.

In order to make adult cells pluripotent without fusing them to embryonic stem cells, regulatory genes that induce pluripotency must be introduced into the nuclei of adult cells. To do this, adult cells are grown in cell culture, and specific combinations of regulatory genes are inserted into retroviruses (viruses that convert RNA into DNA), which are then introduced to the culture medium. The retroviruses transport the RNA of the regulatory genes into the nuclei of the adult cells, where the genes are then incorporated into the DNA of the cells. About 1 out of every 10,000 cells acquires embryonic stem cell properties. Although the mechanism is still uncertain, it is clear that some of the genes confer embryonic stem cell properties by means of the regulation of numerous other genes. Adult cells that become reprogrammed in this way are known as induced pluripotent stem cells (iPS).

Similar to embryonic stem cells, induced pluripotent stem cells can be stimulated to differentiate into select types of cells that could in principle be used for disease-specific treatments. In addition, the generation of induced pluripotent stem cells from the adult cells of patients affected by genetic diseases can be used to model the diseases in the laboratory. For example, in 2008 researchers isolated skin cells from a child with an inherited neurological disease called spinal muscular atrophy and then reprogrammed these cells into induced pluripotent stem cells. The reprogrammed cells retained the disease genotype of the adult cells and were stimulated to differentiate into motor neurons that displayed functional insufficiencies associated with spinal muscular atrophy. By recapitulating the disease in the laboratory, scientists were able to study closely the cellular changes that occurred as the disease progressed.

Such models promise not only to improve scientists' understanding of genetic diseases but also to facilitate the development of new therapeutic strategies tailored to each type of genetic disease.

In 2009 scientists successfully generated retinal cells of the human eye by reprogramming adult skin cells. This advance enabled detailed investigation of the embryonic development of retinal cells and opened avenues for the generation of novel therapies for eye diseases. The production of retinal cells from reprogrammed skin cells may be particularly useful in the treatment of retinitis pigmentosa, which is characterized by the progressive degeneration of the retina, eventually leading to night blindness and other complications of vision. Although retinal cells also have been produced from human embryonic stem cells, induced pluripotency represents a less controversial approach. Scientists have also explored the possibility of combining induced pluripotent stem cell technology with gene therapy, which would be of value particularly for patients with genetic disease who would benefit from autologous transplantation.

Researchers have also been able to generate cardiac stem cells for the treatment of certain forms of heart disease through the process of dedifferentiation, in which mature heart cells are stimulated to revert to stem cells. The first attempt at the transplantation of autologous cardiac stem cells was performed in 2009, when doctors isolated heart tissue from a patient, cultured the tissue in a laboratory, stimulated cell dedifferentiation, and then reinfused the cardiac stem cells directly into the patient's heart. A similar study involving 14 patients who underwent cardiac bypass surgery followed by cardiac stem cell transplantation was reported in 2011. More than three months after stem cell transplantation, the patients experienced a slight but detectable improvement in heart function.

Patient-specific induced pluripotent stem cells are highly valuable in terms of their therapeutic applications because they are unlikely to be rejected by the immune system. However, before induced pluripotent stem cells can be used to treat human diseases, researchers must find a way to introduce the active reprogramming genes without using retroviruses, which can cause diseases such as leukemia in humans. A possible alternative to the use of retroviruses to transport regulatory genes into the nuclei of adult cells is the use of plasmids, which are less tumourigenic than viruses.

CONCLUSION

S tudy of the cell has led to remarkable break-throughs in a wide variety of scientific fields. Gaining a better understanding of the organelles, genes, and proteins within different types of cells and the processes that they facilitate—from membrane transport and signaling to cell division and differentiation—has applications that spread far beyond the cell itself. Cell biology research has led to the development of drugs that can help combat cancers and infectious diseases. Stem cells represent one of the most promising research avenues for treating degenerative diseases, but there are many others, as well. For example, scientists investigating tumour cells often seek to identify specific genetic mutations that give rise to abnormally functioning proteins and thereby promote tumour growth. Meanwhile, research into plant cells has led to improved agricultural techniques that can expand food production worldwide, as well as the development of genetically modified food crops. Continued research into the fundamental unit of life will have broad implications for our understanding of life on Earth.

GLOSSARY

adenosine triphosphate (ATP) An organic compound that is a substrate in many enzyme-catalyzed reactions (catalysis) in the cells of animals, plants, and microorganisms.

apoptosis Programmed cell death; the mechanism that allows cells to self-destruct when stimulated by the appropriate trigger.

chimera In botany, a plant or plant part that is a mixture of two or more genetically different types of cells.

chromosome The microscopic, threadlike part of a cell that carries hereditary information in the form of genes.

cytoplasmic Having to do with the protoplasm of a cell that is external to the nuclear membrane.

cytoskeleton A system of microscopic filaments or fibres, present in the cytoplasm of eukaryotic cells (eukaryote), that organizes other cell components, maintains cell shape, and is responsible for cell locomotion and for movement of the organelles within it.

deoxyribonucleic acid (DNA) One of two types of nucleic acid (the other is RNA); a complex organic compound found in all living cells and many viruses.

endoplasmic reticulum The membrane system within the cytoplasm of a eukaryotic cell (eukaryote). It is important in the synthesis of proteins and lipids.

epigenetics The study of the chemical modification of specific genes or gene-associated proteins of an organism.

eukaryote Any organism composed of one or more

cells, each of which contains a clearly defined nucleus enclosed by a membrane, along with organelles (small, self-contained cellular parts that perform specific functions).

Golgi apparatus   The membrane-bound organelle of eukaryotic cells responsible for transporting, modifying, and packaging proteins and lipids into vesicles for delivery to targeted destinations.

histone   Any of a class of rather simple proteins occurring in cell nuclei and in combination with DNA to form nucleoproteins.

meiosis   The division of a gamete-producing cell in which the nucleus splits twice, resulting in four sex cells (gametes, or eggs and sperm), each possessing half the number of chromosomes of the original cell.

mitochondrion   A membrane-bound organelle located in the cytoplasm of almost all eukaryotic cells, the primary function of which is to generate energy in the form of adenosine triphosphate (ATP).

mitosis   Cell division, or reproduction, in which a cell gives rise to two genetically identical daughter cells.

necrosis   Cell death concerning a circumscribed area of plant or animal tissue that results from an outside cause.

phagocyte   A cell with the ability to ingest, and occasionally digest, foreign particles (e.g., bacteria, carbon, dust, or dye).

phagocytosis   The process by which certain living cells called phagocytes consume or engulf other cells or particles.

phloem Plant tissues that conduct foods made in the leaves to all other parts of the plant.

photosynthesis The process by which green plants and certain other organisms transform light into chemical energy.

pluripotent Capable of differentiating into one of numerous cell types.

prokaryote Any cellular organism that lacks a distinct nucleus.

protoplasm A cell's cytoplasm and nucleus.

ribonucleic acid (RNA) One of the two main types of nucleic acid (the other being DNA), which functions in cellular protein synthesis in all living cells and replaces DNA as the carrier of genetic information in some viruses.

stem cell In living organisms, an undifferentiated cell that can produce other cells that eventually make up specialized tissues and organs.

turgor Pressure exerted by fluid in a cell that presses the cell membrane against the cell wall.

vacuole A space within a cell that is empty of cytoplasm, lined with a membrane, and filled with fluid.

BIBLIOGRAPHY

HISTORY OF CELL THEORY

Classical microscopy and the revelation of the chromosome are discussed in Edmund B. Wilson, *The Cell in Development and Heredity*, 3rd rev. ed. (1925). Max Verworn, *General Physiology: An Outline of the Science of Life* (1899; originally published in German, 2nd ed., 1897), recounts the outlook on the cell at the turn of the 19th century. Sir William Maddock Bayliss, *Principles of General Physiology*, 4th ed. (1924); and Lewis Victor Heilbrunn, *An Outline of General Physiology*, 3rd ed. (1952), are important historical texts tracing the development of the study of cell function in the 20th century.

NATURE AND FUNCTION OF CELLS

Comprehensive works touching on many aspects of the fields of cell biology include Bruce Alberts, *Molecular Biology of the Cell*, 5th ed. (2008), a clear and thorough introduction to the subject; and Harvey F. Lodish, *Molecular Cell Biology*, 7th ed. (2011).

SPECIAL FUNCTIONS OF CELLS

Thomas Zeuthen and Wilfred D. Stein, *Molecular Mechanisms of Water Transport Across Biological Membranes* (2002); David G. Nicholls and S.J. Ferguson, *Bioenergetics 4*, 4th ed. (2013), an exploration of mitochondrial and chloroplastic function; Jean-Paul Thiery (ed.), *Molecular Mechanisms of Transcellular Signaling: From Membrane Receptors to Transcription Factors* (1999); Barbara Young, *Wheater's Functional Histology: A Text and Colour Atlas* (2006), a well-illustrated account of the histology of the human body; and J.M.W. Slack, *From Egg to Embryo: Determinative Events in Early Development*, 2nd ed. (1990).

STRUCTURE OF CELLS

Studies of the form and structure of cells include Peter Lenz, *Cell Motility* (2007); and J. Richard McIntosh, *Cellular Electron Microscopy* (2007).

PLANT CELLS

The biology of plant cells is treated in Ray F. Evert, Peter H. Raven, and Susan E. Eichhorn, *Biology* of Plants, 8th ed. (2013), a general work; and Keith Roberts, *Handbook of Plant Science* (2007).

MEMBRANE CHANNELS

Information on the function and physical and molecular characteristics of ion channels is provided in Bertil Hill, *Ion Channels of Excitable Membranes*, 3rd ed. (2001); and James N.C. Kew and Ceri H. Davies (eds.), *Ion Channels: From Structure to Function* (2010). Shin-Ho Chung, Olaf S. Andersen, and Vikram Krishnamurthy (eds.), *Biological Membrane Ion Channels: Dynamics, Structure, and Applications* (2007), discusses specific types of ion channels and explains their applications in basic research, particularly in the field of biophysics. A work providing extensive, up-to-date information on TRP channels is Veit M. Flockerzi and Bernd Nilius (eds.), *Transient Receptor Potential (TRP) Channels* (2007). Ion channels and their roles in sensory reception are discussed in Boris Martinac, *Sensing with Ion Channels* (2008).

INDEX